SARAJEVO BLUES

Semezdin Mehmedinović

Translated from the Bosnian
and with an Introduction by

Ammiel Alcalay

City Lights Books
San Francisco
1998

Copyright © 1995, 1998 by Semezdin Mehmedinović
Translation copyright © 1998 by Ammiel Alcalay
All Rights Reserved
10 9 8 7 6 5 4 3 2 1

Originally published by Durieux in Zagreb by Nenad Popović under
the title *Sarajevo Blues* as part of the EX PONTO series which is
edited by Ivan Lovrenović.

Cover design by DiJiT
Book design by Robert Sharrard
Typography by Harvest Graphics

Author photo copyright © Gerard Rondeau
Reproduced by courtesy of Gerard Rondeau

Library of Congress Cataloging-in-Publication Data

Mehmedinović, Semezdin, 1960-
     (Sarajevo blues.   English)
     Sarajevo blues / by Semezdin Mehmedinović ; translated
from the Bosnian by Ammiel Alcalay.
        p.   cm.
     ISBN 0-87286-345-X
     I. Alcalay, Ammiel. II. Title.
     PG1619.23.E464S2713   1998
     891.8'236—dc21   98-33738
                                              CIP

City Lights Books are available to bookstores through our primary
distributor: Subterranean Company, P. O. Box 160, 265 S. 5th St.,
Monroe, OR 97456. Tel: (541)-847-5274. Toll-free orders
(800)-274-7826. Fax: (541)-847-6018. Our books are also available
through library jobbers and regional distributors. For personal orders
and catalogs, please write to City Lights Books, 261 Columbus
Avenue, San Francisco, CA 94133, or visit us on the World Wide
Web at: www.citylights.com.

CITY LIGHTS BOOKS are edited by Lawrence Ferlinghetti and
Nancy J. Peters and published at the City Lights Bookstore,
261 Columbus Avenue, San Francisco, CA 94133.

Contents

TRANSLATOR'S INTRODUCTION
"PRACTICING FOR THE LAST WORD"

The creation of a receptive space for marginalized literatures or languages can occur through a variety of means. Unfortunately, in far too many instances, war and conflict become the primary means through which an unperturbed or disinterested audience connects to places far removed from the orbit of their ordinary aesthetic, formal, existential or political concerns. Bosnian writing is certainly a case in point. Prior to the war in the former Yugoslavia, the few ex-Yugoslav writers known in the United States tended to be those either promoted or shunned by the Yugoslav state's centralized cultural apparatus. Thus, American readers might be familiar with the names of Ivo Andrić (Yugoslavia's only Nobel Prize recipient) on the one hand, and Danilo Kiš on the other. Andrić, a Croat excluded from the Croatian canon, wrote primarily about Bosnia and was embraced, usually for all the wrong reasons, by nationalist Serbs. Kiš, on the other hand, was all but disowned by his own country only to be adopted into the wave of Eastern European "dissident" writing, so popular in the United States during the 1970s and 1980s. In both cases, American readers barely caught a glimpse of the enormously complex relationships both of these writers had with conflicting versions of history, both past and to be written, as well as to intertwined linguistic, communal, national and regional allegiences. Unquestionably, such a simplified picture of received cultural history—of which the above is only one small example — played a significant role in the information gap obfuscating the real issues at stake in the wars of the former Yugoslavia, and prolonged the lack of resolve by those with power to act decisively in ending them.

At the beginning of the war against Bosnia-Hercegovina, I found myself spontaneously translating texts that I came across in the Bosnian press. When I tried to place them in magazines or journals, I found an almost unanimous unwillingness to cede power in the form of allowing Bosnian voices to appear in print at the same time that these same outlets were flooded with reports and impressions of sojourners, most of whom didn't even speak the language. As the siege continued, I found myself the designated clearing-house for almost anything and everything published during the war. As I began to work on texts more clearly literary in form, I realized that creating space for the reception of such works would, indeed, mean going in for the long haul. I was reminded of my inability, in the 1980s when Eastern European "dissident" writing was the operating code, to interest any publisher in the since translated Bosnian classic *Death and the Dervish*, by Meša Selimović. Had it not been for the war and the extraordinary attention it got, this book probably never would have found an American publisher, an irony lost on a literary public that too often has very little sense of what is actually going on in the rest of the world while purporting to be at the center of it.

Although it can leave one stranded, translation is — by definition — a collective endeavor. Creating space for a Bosnian point of view meant, primarily, working with and through friends to push through doors that had begun to crack open. It was through such connections that I first heard about the work of Semezdin Mehmedinović and his remarkable war time collection *Sarajevo Blues*. The version that I got was sent to me by Josip Osti from Slovenia, where it was the first book to come out in his Biblioteka "egzil-abc" series. Published in Ljubljana, these books provided a forum for Bosnian writers and translators, either under siege or in exile, to continue publishing their work. Situated between an immensity of pain and the perverse magnitude of the resources the mass media had at their disposal, the books themselves were "small" productions: 4 x 6 inches, they ran between twenty and seventy pages, and were printed in editions of between one hundred and two hundred copies. Each book had a lower-case letter on the cover, indicating its order in the series. When you actually have a copy of one of these books in your hand, you begin to understand what Semezdin Mehmedinović means when he writes that "writing is, finally, quite a personal thing that doesn't make much sense unless you are practicing for the *last word*."

Semezdin Mehmedinović was born in 1960 in Kiseljak, near the city of Tuzla. As stated in the biographical notes to his second book, *Emigrant*, published in 1990, "like all people from Tuzla who don't like Sarajevo," he did, indeed, move to Sarajevo where he finished a degree in Comparative Literature and Library Science, completed his obligatory service in the then Yugoslav National Army, and became active in the thriving Sarajevo cultural and countercultural scene. Sarajevo in the late 1970s and 1980s was characterized by an extremely original and innovative rock music scene that both influenced and interacted with traditional and not so traditional art forms including performance, theater, film, comic art, the visual arts and literature.

While Mehmedinović did a stint as secretary of the Translator's Union, a more traditional role for an aspiring writer with a degree from the Philosophy Faculty in a socialist country, he found himself—more often than not—working at the kinds of jobs one would more typically associate with a writer in America than the Yugoslavia of that time, with its highly bureaucratized and privilege driven literary hierarchy. The reason for this, of course, had to do with Mehmedinović's activities as an editor of two of the more interesting cultural journals of the period, one of which, *Valter*, was eventually censored. His first book, *Modrac*, was published by Svjetlost in Sarajevo in 1984, and won the Trebinje Award for a first book of poetry. By the time his second book came out in 1990, Mehmedinović was working as a bartender. His work, like a number of other writers of his generation, seemed to foreshadow things to come. This can be hinted at in "Zenica Blues," one of the strongest poems of the late 1980s in that collection.

In 1991, Mehmedinović was one of the founders of a new journal called *Phantom of Liberty*, three isssues of which came out prior to the war, and three during the siege. The ability of Sarajevo's artistic community to resist the genocidal attack of Serbian nationalists through cultural production and public activity in a city deprived, literally, of any safe public or private space, has almost become a cliché. Clearly,

Mehmedinović's work on *Phantom of Liberty* represents a model of this, from the group of talented young people involved to its high production values and biting visual and textual commentaries. Remaining in Sarajevo throughout the war with his family, Mehmedinović continued to work on *Phantom of Liberty*, and as a freelance journalist, filmscript writer and poet. A film that he wrote the script for and co-directed with Benjamin Filipović, *Leaving-Am-I or the End of Theater*, was shown at the Berlin film festival in 1994 and awarded first prize at the Mediterranean film festival in Rome in 1995. An expanded version of *Sarajevo Blues* was published in Zagreb, also in 1995.

Ironically, until the point of utter exhaustion after more than four years under siege, Mehmedinović was enormously productive within the new, more clarified political circumstances and allegiences created by the war. The fact that Mehmedinović was not particularly comfortable in the good old former Yugoslavia clearly marks the critical ability of his work to probe many of the more false and corrosive assumptions underlying the old structures while never for a moment romanticizing the "west." This positioning, along with his relentless examination of issues involving media imagery and representation, forms a remarkably cogent critique—from the other side—of some of the more facile claims and assumptions of "post-modernism." When he writes, as in the prose poem "Grenade," it is with more than some authority: "What kind of curriculum will be put in place for kids ripped apart by shrapnel as sharp as razors? Imagine a teacher assigning "Snail House" or "The

Enchanted Saddle." It's easier to think of war as their only school. And there are plenty of shells, they're so devastating that only the Schwartzeneggers have a chance to survive — at least according to post-modern theorists — left to themselves, wandering naked through the global desert and the infosphere, new nomads freed from feudal prejudice, not as members of a nation but as carriers of information they'll exchange between themselves together in the planetary community."

Poetry is also information and in translating such work we take both the risk and the responsibility of giving these words another life, of turning what Mehmedinović refers to as the "last word" into "literature," and providing their possessors a path — however tenuous — back into an indifferent world such words no longer seem to have anything to do with. After a number of years working in and on cultures, languages and bodies of writing that have been neglected or marginalized for a variety of reasons, it is quite clear to me that writing which isn't read and absorbed by other writers into the possibilities of their own work is destined to remain just another consumable item, as easy to laud as it is to discard. Once commodified, such work is also neutralized and loses almost all its transformative or political power. And by political I also mean the effect any event can have on consciousness itself, one of our most primal forms of self-governance. Such an event can also be a reading that forever alters our assumptions about someone else's experience. The implications of this, it seems to me, are profound. My own experiences translating texts from

Bosnia during and after the war has proven most instructive in this regard. I would like to think that much of what I have done in this area can be considered literary activism. I find too many of my contemporaries taking up modes of theoretical writing that purport to have serious political or cultural implications but seem more like new forms of colonialism in which "subjects"—whether these be writers, artists or others—become natives subjugated to a disturbingly reductive vocabulary. In retrospect, I believe my decision to use translation as a field of activity harbors more radical possibilities than I might even have originally considered. Rather than a passive conduit, the translator is often an alchemist and healer of wounds in the sense conjured up by Wilson Harris when he speaks of the pain engendered by "phantom limbs," the severed traces of which we must dig very deep to find. The translator's search for words and the unexplored correspondences they might contain—as narrative, context, and irreducible difference —is part of this expedition into ourselves and our relationship to other worlds that remains such a crucial part of at least attempting to preserve the civility in civilization.

During the process of my own education in and on Bosnia, there are many, many people that I crossed paths with and who, in either a fleeting moment or an ongoing relationship, provided answers, more questions, help, information and materials; others were either instrumental in paving the way for works from Bosnia to be appear in this country or simply helped in any way they could. I would like to thank Želimir Altarac, Jo Andres, Martim Avillez,

Aleš Debeljak, Zlatko Dizdarević, Ferida Duraković, Paul Golub, Paula Gordon, Izeta Gradjević, Viktor Ivančić, Ken Jordan, Nebojša Jovanović, Suada Kapić, Ozren Kebo, Ademir Kenović, Salko Krijestorac, Josip Osti, Amir Pašić, Senad Pećanin, Miro Purivatra, Nada and Mirsad Selimović, Abdulah Sidran, Mirsad Sijarić, Susan Sontag, Thomas Thornton, Goran Tomčić, Marko Vešović, Srdjan Vuletić, Aleksandra Wagner and Leon Wieseltier. Thanks are due to editors and journals where some of these texts first appeared; to Scott Malcomson at the *Village Voice*, for making things possible; Bradford Morrow at *Conjunctions*; Gil Ott at *High Performance*; Yasemin Yaldiz and the editorial collective at *Found Object*; Kenneth Brown and Hannah Davis at *Mediterraneans*; and Chris Agee as editor of the anthology *Scar on the Stone*. I would also particularly like to thank Ivan Lovrenović, a profound intellectual and a truly cultured person who has consistently provided, by example, a "third way." As always, Bob Sharrard of City Lights has been enormously supportive and helpful, and I would like to thank him again. I would also like to acknowledge the support of the National Endowment of the Arts which awarded me with a translation fellowship for my work on Bosnian writing; finally, I would also like to acknowledge the support of a PSC-CUNY grant for my work on Bosnia.

NOTE ON PRONOUNCIATION

Names of people and places have been left in their original transcription: "c" (as in "Grbavica"), is pronounced "ts" (as in "cats"); "č" and "ć" (as in Kovačević) are hard and soft versions of "ch" (as in "chain"); "š" (as in Lapišnica) is pronounced "sh" (as in "ship"); "ž" not preceded by "d" (as in Željo), is pronounced like the "g" in the French word "gendarme;" if preceded by "d" (as in Karadžić), it is pronounced as a hard "j" (as in "jar"); "j" (as in Miljacka) is pronounced "y" (as in "yet") or (as in Bajram) as long"ay" (as in "icon").

LOSS

I remember how—on my first reading—Goethe's *Der Erlkönig* really got to me: the part about the father holding the dying child in his arms. The magnitude of the child's fear and the father's powerlessness made my hair stand on end! I've thought of that poem so many times this past year, and not because the feelings it once evoked come back to me again and again in this reality permeated by the presence of death. Rather because death was so present that I couldn't identify it through a specific tragedy. I invoked the feeling to induce my own sense of *the tragic*.

All in all, that was just a sham. The essence of poetry is that we experience the words of a poem as if informed within us, or as if we ourselves had uttered them. From this it becomes possible to identify with the tragic in Goethe's classical construction. It looks like the war controls our sorrow, holding it in reserve for those dear or close to us . . .

Very few people haven't had something happen to them. Everyone keeps their distance from those whose tragedies are *fresher*. That's why I feel uneasy writing about my own loss, but I write from a pressure deep within.

My father died. Not here, he was in another city under siege, in Northern Bosnia. I love him as much as a son loves a father and I still haven't gotten used to the feeling that he's gone. I put off my encounter with his death and, now, when I think of him, the images that come to me are joyous and sad, innocent.

He hardly ever got sick. Once he had tonsilitis that got

infected: I can see him contorting his eyeballs to have a full view of the mirror while I—following his directions— blow ammonium chloride over his swollen tonsils through a plastic straw. This is one of the first things that comes to mind and every time I remember, I smile. And this protects me from attacks of melancholy, it holds my balance.

He was a miner, and he possessed a perfect sense of simplicity in showing his feelings. He couldn't be counted amongst the *strong*. He displayed his weakness so easily that I often felt the need to hug him. For instance, I started buying cigarettes quite early. As soon as I began, he started buying them too: he was like someone who thought he'd missed out on something and had to race to make up for it— like someone who measured out his own years according to the growth of his son.

I can't let myself think of him that way now because I'm afraid I'd just fall apart. The war created a dual selfishness in me: I'm shaken by a death that has taken place far from here, and I'm quenched by the death in this city that only fills me with a dull sense of dread. The other part of my selfishness has to do with delaying an encounter with my father's death. Like yesterday when I avoided telling him something that I knew I had to tell him so that, obstinately, it remains *unsaid*. And this that is *unsaid* gets to me, and that's why I call upon images of plain happiness.

With sharp pruning shears my father cuts the dry limbs in the warm April afternoon and sings *Hey, I'm cutting the pearly apple . . .*

•

He keeps ringing until I get up
And when he comes in he looks at the paper on the table.
No inspiration? My father asks.
Look—he says—the lake is so frozen
That heavy trucks can go over it
If they have chains on their winter tires.
He keeps talking until I'm convinced the
World can be looked at from another perspective
And I see people walking across the lake
Each one with a fish-hook in their mouth.

I ask myself
Which one of us will die first?
But only after he took off his jacket
to show the two bites of a clothespin
on the shoulders of his white shirt.

SINGULAR DREAM

The bike hitched up on his back, my father
        adjusts the chain, not lifting his head.
A lot of people putter around the yard.
Are these dead, dad?
Don't worry, son, you can play
        with them.
Ants hide from the huge blackberries,
        under my heel.
The rocker, empty, rises to the sky
        and falls.
In yellow raincoats, they are looking for
        a way out of the garden.
They look at me, but just over their shoulders.
One comes to the fence, grabbing the door knob,
        but it isn't there, the door isn't.
Twenty years ago, remember father,
        there were gates here.

CORPSE

We slowed down at the bridge
to watch some dogs tear a
corpse apart by the river
and then we went on

nothing in me has changed

I heard the crunch of snow under tires
like teeth biting into an apple
and felt the wild desire to laugh
at you
because you call this place hell
and you flee from here convinced
that death outside Sarajevo does not exist

AUGUST, 1989

The synagogue at night.
Rain outside.
I'm already making coffee for the third time.
An old poet dozes off on the floor
Covered in a flag.

Ah, poor old poet
Curled up like a foetus
Wrapped up in the state flag
Sleeping.

THE PHONE RINGS

The phone keeps ringing.
I go to look out the window
and an eyelash falls in my eye.
Everything seems sluggish and wobbly
and no one knows what they're doing
par for the course in this
social-realist paradise.

Maybe everyone except the fence
on the bridge with his gold watch
getting ready to pick up
some perfume for his girl
riding a Vespa all the way to Istanbul.

IN THE STUDIO

We're sitting on logs in the studio.
The only women here are on paper.
Crumbs of hashish from Afghanistan
dot the sharp tips of a small pair of scissors.
A guy on the balcony in the house across
the way is pulling an arc welder apart in the dark.
We're sitting on logs in the studio
and everything is so peaceful.
All that will change
as soon as I get into my pajamas.
It's cold out.
We're surrounded by mountains
filled with the mournful howl of chain saws.

ALIFAKOVAC

At the very eastern edge of Sarajevo
a boy loaded down with an armful of roses —

It's *Bajram* and he, the little merchant,
is going to the graveyard loaded with roses

loaded with a hundred course roses
like a grave on the day of its digging

Like a grave on the day of its digging
the boy is climbing Alifakovac

STRANGER

Once I too will depart alone
into the darkness of the grave —
on Alifakovac
or another hill, the city
I knew everyone in
and now only two or
three remain —
and only night, alone
I look out from the past
on the city's darkness
from someone else's
home, I, stranger —
I a stranger

ESSAY

This evening walk deserves a poem.
A plane gleaming over the suburbs
Sinks into the bluish dusk.
Wires spark over the trollies.
A woman who lost her earring
Comes back up the street looking for it.
Feel sorrow for her suddenly.
For the boy looking at himself
In the bell of his bicycle.
For the old man on the bridge, waving to me:
"How is it possible that a river can dry up
in this best of all possible worlds?"
Finally
For the pattern of freckles
On my mother's face
While she assures me as we walk
That God is wherever I think of him.

DESERTER

Only then —
not before you have coffee
at the train station;
the dispatcher tapping the wheels
of the locomotive with a hammer;
the paper tucked under your arm —
leaving the city in peace —
you'll never be true to yourself anywhere
unless your very life is the only truth
unless the empty air calls itself freedom —
unless you're a deserter
with an uneasy conscience
unless you're Billy the Kid

SPIRITUALITY

In the evening we wait for
the moment forms open:
the sky is still in darkness
from the radiance of earthly things —
and then the buildings become like models
blackened by the shadow of their surfaces
and the torrid sky appears
as the moon begins to shine amidst the war —

That instant everything —
and my son looking out the window —
casts a divine smile
on the domesticated power of the elements

STOCKING HAT

The war started on Sunday. I know this because we always
played soccer at Skenderija on Sunday. A guy from my team
didn't show up that night but no one paid much attention to
it. After the game we went out, as always, for a beer. When
it came time for the last trolley, I got ready to head home. It
happened to be a short ride because a bunch of guys with
stockings over their heads and kalashnikovs aimed at us
stopped the trolley. As I got out, I took a look at this motley
crew only to recognize the guy from my team who hadn't
shown up. I was so taken by surprise that I had to repeat my
question twice: "Šljuka, is that you?" Embarrassed, he just
kept quiet behind his stocking.

My confusion lasted for a while. Instead of a guy I was
supposed to hang out with over a few beers after a game, I
found myself facing a real terrorist occupying the very
trolley I happened to be riding in. I couldn't figure out how
to explain this to myself, this fundamental physiognomic
change. But when the number of people began to
multiply—the number of people who, like Šljuka, started
wearing stockings on their heads instead of their feet—I
was no longer confused.

The next day, after the trolley incident, I heard Radovan
Karadžić on the news. Every now and then his voice came
from off-camera as the screen filled with scenes from the
previous day, among them a shot of the gang with stockings
over their heads standing in front of the halted trolley.
Karadžić spouted such blatant lies that, in a rage, I found a

book of his children' poetry—*There Are Miracles, There Are No Miracles,* and began ripping it apart. My son protested so much (he actually threw a fit before my very eyes, even though he himself was scared watching the news), that I stopped, somewhat bewildered. I started taping together the ripped pages, to calm down a little boy whose world was being destroyed by grown-ups, a fact he refused to acknowledge. My son knew the author of this book, and he couldn't let himself believe such a man would want to harm him.

I knew him too, from before the war. He wrote poems that no one in our crowd really thought too much of. I certainly didn't. Having faith in my son's taste, however, I had to give my nod of approval to his poetry for children. Karadžić himself was quite aware of the fact that no one thought he had much talent as a writer, but in meeting him it wasn't easy to detect either bitterness or, for that matter, the kind of vanity writers usually possess. On the contrary, in all of our meetings he seemed to present very reasonable suggestions and no one really suspected that he would be a future candidate for political office. He seldom spoke when we hung out in a group at cafes, he just listened. When he did join a conversation, his words were calm and reassuring, perhaps because of his years as a psychiatrist. But no one remembered Radovan Karadžić's poems, and the hatred so evident in his early poetry just slipped by, even though his line "Take no pity let's go / kill that scum in the city" became a slogan for the war project.

Despite everything, Karadžić gave the impression of a

peace-loving and good-natured fellow. During the first multi-party elections, after the fall of socialism, he founded the Greens. That seemed quite in character. Founding such a party, given conditions in the Balkans, represented more of an artistic performance than true political engagement. The Greens first action in Sarajevo proved this: they draped plastic bags in various colors over the boughs of the acacias lining some of Sarajevo's main streets. Not too many months after this, he became the leader of the Serb nationalists. In order to fit his new role, he deliberately held his left hand off to the side so that inquisitive onlookers could see the handle of his pistol tucked under his jacket. The transformation was fundamental. Only Radovan had no need to put a stocking over his head for this change in physiognomy to become apparent: his expression turned wild and he was no longer the same person I had once known. His unassuming look evaporated, like the soul leaving the body of a dead man.

A number of writers, his contempoararies, now claim Radovan always displayed criminal behavior; in other words, it wasn't, as I sometimes thought, a question of fundamental metamorphosis. On the contrary, they were ready to testify that Karadžić always showed signs of his malicious nature, try as he might to cover up for it. A.S. showed me scars on his forearms that served as testimony to the following incident: after realizing Radovan might have reported on his private conversations (it was certainly true that the state appeared to know even the most intimate thoughts of an individual, such were the times), A.S.

extinguished cigarettes on his own skin in an attempt—
through his own pain—to get Karadžić to admit to his role
as an informer for the secret police.

Looking at things from this perspective, the belief that
someone else's pain might gain the sympathy of a future war
criminal seems pretty lame. But that incident, from the early
'70s, demands further explanation. The generation Radovan
Karadžić happened to form a part of was destined to be
marked by the events of 1968. Student unrest in Sarajevo
was rather mild and quite removed from the resounding
volleys of global revolution but the authorities, neverthe-
less, almost instantly set about coopting the most vocal
protestors for their own purposes. They were given positions
in various ministries or else simply put on the payroll of
the internal security services; the authorities figured their
revolutionary potential would find a proper outlet in the
long run. This is how the political opposition first turned
into paid informers before—as they passed their time in the
lap of luxury—turning into greedy scumbags. The student
demonstrations of '68 found Karadžić on the street where,
just as before the war—because of a greed that truly
surprised me—he turned to crime. He even spent a year in
jail. By then it was already clear that the docility he
displayed in speaking to his literary contemporaries was a
farce. And someone who was prepared to steal wouldn't
have far to go in order to kill. Karadžić followed through
this sequence with flying colors.

Socialism's kids that liked to dress up preferred Lenin-
style hats while Karadžić's "poetic" generation was

obsessed with Russian culture. One inherited trait—to take the revolution as the measure of every event—probably had a lot to do with Radovan Karadžić's candidacy as a contractor of war works. As long as there was revolutionary change: even if it came about through sheer pillage and plunder, even if it came about through absolute terror. If robbery was involved, so much the better. These were the criteria that made him the perfect errand-boy for Milošević's nationalist-Stalinist project.

When I look back on the days of Karadžić's 'anti-militarism', from the time he was a founder of the Greens, those plastic bags stick in my mind as one of the war's most dominant objects. The refugees that this poet expelled from their homes carried only what could fit in a plastic bag. Photos and video-clips from the war in Bosnia are full of those plastic bags, to the point that this harmless object turned into a precise picture of the tragedy, its very metaphor.

I've never thought much of dwelling on someone else's deeds in retrospect. Looking at things that way says more about the person remembering than the person who actually did the deed. I rarely thought of Karadžić during the war; I was much more occupied with the problem of simply surviving. Only on days when things in Sarajevo became truly intolerable did I remember that my life had been made unbearable through Karadžić's will. There were, unfortunately, more than enough days like that but I remember one in particular. Not because it was the most horrible, since it wasn't, but probably because it made me think of Radovan *underground*.

I was coming back to the city the only way you could get back to Sarajevo: through the tunnel. Water seeped in everywhere through the narrow passageway beneath the runway at the airport and the mud made it even harder to get through. The tunnel was so narrow that I felt like I was about to have a head on collision with the oranges that were being shuttled into the city on little wagons all night long. Since there wasn't enough air, I became so exhausted that I had to stop half-way. I didn't have the strength to take another step forward but I had already gone too far to turn back. I was ready to just lay down and die right where I was until I found a spot that was a little wider (now I think that spot must have been made to put aside the dead, so the living could pass). I just stayed right there, for hours, underground, and thought of Radovan. We were in the Writer's Club one summer afternoon and he was telling me, with great enthusiasm, about a movie he had seen the day before. The movie was *Sophie's Choice*, and Radovan, speaking from the professional perspective of someone concerned with the human psyche, interpreted in great detail the various aspects of Meryl Streep's spiritual state in the scene where a German officer presents her with the following choice: which of her two children should be saved, since one would have to be killed. Underground, my hair stood on end as I remembered his rational analysis of Sophie's choice.

Radovan's psychiatric war strategy was given a truly terrifying name by the leader of his army, General Ratko Mladić: "mind-bending," they called it. This "mind-bending" consisted of the relentless humiliation of innocent people, and it was only in my own submission underground that I fully saw his intention. The ghastly scene from *Sophie's Choice* was endlessly repeated in Bosnia: Karadžić's soldiers put mothers in the same position in which Meryl Streep found herself in the cinematic reconstruction of events that took place in a German concentration camp.

Karadžić must have derived at least some pleasure from the pain of his literary companion, the guy who put cigarettes out on his own forearms; somewhere in his mind, he must already have conjured up some of the *hellish* intentions that would be realized during the war. I use the adjectival form here intentionally because the reality of the war in Bosnia as created by Radovan Karadžić for the media has too often been called *hell*—as if our Bosnia were static, and not subject to change.

At the beginning of the war, a photograph appeared in the Sarajevo daily *Oslobodjenje*. There was a building in flames, spewing forth billows of thick, black smoke. Right when the photograph was taken, the smoke formed a clearly recognizable image of Radovan Karadžić. The very man who put the city to flames now appeared through the smoke like a devil overseeing his own destructive acts. There was no escaping it, everyone who saw the picture had precisely the same image in mind. It seems like people can only describe evil by using symbolic language. Even when the smoke over the flaming city appeared in the form of the very person who had set it on fire, that is, as a real person, it could still only be described as the devil's work. A defense mechanism: if this is the work of the devil, then it's not part of this world and evil remains distant.

The war has made me suspicious of any metaphors (and not only because poets turned into murderers). I put even less faith in metaphors derived from religious mythology: things belonging to "that" world, a world that can only be reached by passing through death, no longer concern the living. Thus, all responsibility for the commission of evil can be abdicated. If you follow through on this metaphor—and that is why it always made me uncomfortable—then you can remove any trace of responsibility from Karadžić's *hellish* acts.

That is how, to put it mildly, lies emerged victorious—and were measured out in drums of "non-Serbian" blood. Lies were the only political means in which Radovan Karadžić had absolute faith. Since everything he did in the name of racial "cleanliness" created a fact, so to speak—he was creating a reality to fit his lies—all he had left to do was keep repeating the lies until his accumulated acts made his lies seem irrefutable. Maybe that's why it became so easy for so many of our "neighbors" to put stockings over their heads. The claim most often repeated by Karadžić—that people of different nationalities couldn't live together in Bosnia—was simply a euphemism for racism. The truth was quite the opposite: peoples of different cultures had lived together for so long in Bosnia, and the ethnic mix was so deep, that any separation could only be accomplished through extreme violence and enormous bloodshed.

It was right during the period when Karadžić was the

most vocal champion of absolute separation along "cultural border-lines" that I happened to thumb through the 1991/92 Sarajevo phonebook. Under the family name *Karadžić*, I found twenty-one entries. In addition to the aforementioned poet, the rest of the entries could be fit under the following ethnic rubrics: 10 Muslims, 9 Serbs and 1 Croat. The most curious aspect of these lisings is the fact that the only Croat, Mate Karadžić, carried the same first name as the leader of the Croatian nationalist party, Mate Boban. And amongst the Muslims, I found Ale Karadžić, Ale being a term of endearment for Alija, the first name of the Bosnian President Alija Izetbegović.

On the basis of such a Bosnian ethnic inventory, any racist idea—of necessity—becomes grotesque. The most horrendous demonstration of this took place outside of Bosnia, upon the ruins of the small Croatian city of Vukovar. Vojislav Šešelj (who happens to be the only Serb with such a name since all the other Šešeljs are Croats!), celebrated his victory over the city along with his soldiers by feasting on pork. He took the opportunity to tell news reporters that the pigs they were now eating had just fed on the remains of slaughtered Croats.

As opposed to Šešelj, Karadžić only verged on cannibalism in his pronouncements. But even though he himself never crossed the line into actual cannibalism, there was something truly barbaric in his way of thinking and his method of waging war. One of my friends, the writer A.I., used the term "The Devils From Pale." I understood the reasoning behind his use of a capital "D," but the phrase never seemed precise to me. And I also thought that it embodied the typical sense of exasperation displayed by victims in the face of their persecutors, a kind of displaced sense of awe. I think the closest anyone ever got to describing the men from Pale was that boy who became so upset when I ripped his book of children's poetry. He told me a terrific story about how Chetniks multiply, like gremlins, when they come into contact with plum brandy. He managed to translate evil into a comprehensible, childish idiom. After he told me this story, I often caught him poring over maps. He was very interested in Greenland. When I asked why he wanted to go there, he replied: "Cause there's no people there."

I myself no longer have any illusions about people. I know that someone I've just spent a nice afternoon with could knock on my door at any second with a stocking on his head, just the way Stojan Šljuka knocked on the door of the trolley. I haven't seen him since but the wrap-up for the play-by-play from those days was quite gruesome. Vojislav Maksimović, a professor of Yugoslav literature, used the decapitated head of a Muslim as a soccer ball. So I don't have any illusions left about people or, for that matter, about nations. That's why I don't think a single nation exists that wouldn't crucify Christ. In Bosnia, it was Karadžić's Serbs who did the crucifying. It is not only my world that has been deconstructed but language as well. A library, for example, is no longer a building filled with books but a burnt out ruin. These days, if I ever find myself in a library and wander over into the children's section, my heart freezes.

BACK THEN

Today I remembered a greek poet
six feet tall
we sat in Europe, the pinko restaurant,
and talked
he was sentenced to death once
and stayed up till morning waiting for the firing squad
a lot of time has passed since then
now he is manolis anagnostakis
smoking strong greek cigarettes with white filters
and begging off hard liquor
I have the feeling that he's renounced politics
and when we heard an explosion from the sidewalk
and the six foot tall body
leaned over to the window like an arch
someone threw a firecracker into a container
which lit some computer paper
thrown in from the bank across the street on fire
"and I thought not again in Sarajevo"
the words he said sounded like such a crock
alright I thought
anyone who's looked death in the eyes
has the right to play around with it a little
I was young then and I didn't know
that death's something a lot more common than it seems
so plain
        that anything you say about it sounds trite

AT THE EDGE OF TOWN

At the edge of town you can see
a truck left over from the last war
getting smaller down between the poplars.
A prisoner with crumbs in his beard
is pulled out of a military jeep.
Piled up in the warehouse plank by plank
as neat as a sonnet.

At the very edge of town you can see
a biker at full tilt grab at the roof of a long
shack with VULCANIZER written across it.
And many other images rich in madness
to any objective, celestial gaze.
Like the roofs of the houses by the airport
painted in red and white checkerboard squares.

THE CHETNIK POSITION

First a bulldozer came to dig trenches in the ground, then the truck hauling cement blocks to shore them up. Tanks are dug in at the side with just the barrels veering out. And rocket-launchers. Beyond the range of our rifles. Maybe you could even spend the winter in trenches like that. It's August now: tobacco comes in from Niš, and plum brandy from Prokuplje. I don't know where the women come from, but I saw them too, through my binoculars. One of them put an air mattress down by the trench to sun herself in a bathing suit. She lies like that for hours. Then she gets up, goes to the rocket launcher, pulls the catch and lets a shell fly at random toward the city. She listens for a second, looking towards the source of the explosion: she stretches on the tips of her toes, innocently. Then she goes back, rubbing her body in suntan oil to fully give in to her own state of well-being.

EXPULSION

The Chetniks banished the mental patients from Jagomir to the city. That day, one of them—holding the body of a dead sparrow by its claws—came up to someone walking along King Tomislav Street and said: "You'll be dead too, when my army gets here."

CISTERNS / RAINWATER

There's no water: the few water trucks circling the city are immediately assaulted as soon as they pull into a side street, surrounded by a patchwork of canisters and people whose idiosyncracies have reached cosmic proportions. Not one water truck passes without a fight. Real skirmishes develop, with militant women entering the fray, like the old lady standing off to the side without a canister and repeating: "Brothers, Muslims, what are you doing?" Then the rain comes down, as one calamity takes the place of another. Rain drips throughout the house, like from a cistern: the most astute cut their gutters to use as channels for gathering water into basins. The rainwater has already filled the craters blasted out of the asphalt by grenades. The war is entering its preposterous phase: the authorities simply won't be able to deal with so much rainwater.

A RELATIVELY CALM DAY

1)   In the daily reports — when dozens of shells hit "downtown proper," when "snipers are in action" at the intersections and only a few have been killed or wounded — we are informed that a *relatively calm day* has passed. People are relatively normal, or relatively loony since death has been accepted as a statistic. That is to say, in Sarajevo, the issue is a surplus of death.

2)   A flustered young man begs to cut into the water line. He shows his plastic canister. The line in front of the cistern twists to make a place for him. Since he's already loaded his canister, he hurries to the end of the street and gets hit by a grenade. All that's left of him is a bloody trail on the pavement that seems like sap but is easier to clean. Just then, it starts raining and everything gets washed away: not even a trace of the young guy is left, nor a trace of the canister. Just water. As if nothing in the street changed, except that everyone got just a bit quieter. The motor of the water truck rumbles to the sound of plastic canisters softly bumping against each other.

NO MAN'S LAND

For over a month now, over where the dividing line is, the bodies of the dead lie. You can't get close to them; the white UNPROFOR transporters don't go there to pick them up: the unburied lie and their souls wander with the city crows.

CROWS

I remember a reading one night. Miroslav Toholj, my friend at the time, had just come from Bor (where he had also been on literary business), and was still filled with impressions of his trip. He told us of a town in which "the crows didn't survive." Just like that, ecologically beside himself, he spoke of death as if it wasn't a natural phenomenon. This was right before he read a section of *Heartmaster*, a novel of his that had just come out.

At my house early the next morning, my mother was making us breakfast when my son, still drowsy, appeared at the door in his pajamas. Toholj slipped a pencil and a notebook into his hand in which there was a single sentence written: "Bor is a city in which crows can't survive." And, while my son was drawing potato head people, the owner of the notebook brushed his fingers through my son's hair.

The whole incident would be completely irrelevant if the scene hadn't repeated itself today: I'm sitting next to my son, completely engrossed in his drawing, and brushing my fingers through his hair.

After everything that's happened in the meantime, the repetition of this situation—and even my recollection of what took place six years ago—is almost comical. There was real warmth in Miroslav Toholj's gesture, a man who, not long after that visit, would fully devote himself to the expulsion of a whole people. That's what time was like, along with the things occupying it, that it made the feelings connected to any memory seem worthless.

Now, when I think of the Serbian novelist Miroslav Toholj, I am deeply aware that people aren't deserving of tragedy because existence is exalted in and of itself, and brings its own consolation. But people don't deserve consolation. Comedy is closer to the truth, since it at least shows the meaninglessness of things.

From this perspective, knowing that there is a town in which crows can't survive is truly absurd.

And look how the story ends: sitting with my son and brushing my fingers through his hair, I discover a detail that, at first, makes me smile — like when you see a kid wearing the boots of a grown up. As I slowly brush my fingers through my ten year old's hair, I find strands of grey.

GRBAVICA

1)   A part of town in Sarajevo, momentarily under Chetnik occupation. How can Grbavica be Serbia, when a Željo fan—the number one Sarajevo soccer team—an old guy wearing a black beret, said on TV: "We're not butchers, we're just a quiet, aggravating pain in the ass at the starting gate."

2)   The snipers, at least those aiming at Sniper Alley, shoot from the Jewish cemetary. Covered by the gravestones, they're secu (I almost said *secure*, a word I'm not too crazy about, because of State Security, I guess), and safe. Dear Lord, punish all those who desecrate Jewish graves. And punish me, if it was a sin that I picked violets there when I was young.

A MARTYR'S RESTING PLACE

A body just about to be buried. I see a soldier on his knees:
still a kid. His rifle rests in his lap. You can hear the guttural
murmur of Arabic. Sorrow gathers in circles under the eyes;
the men pass their open palms across their faces. As the rites
continue, I feel the presence of God in everything; when this
is over, I will take a pen and make a list of my sins. Now
everything in me resists death: as my tongue passes over my
teeth I can sense the taste of a woman's lipstick. No one is
crying. I keep quiet. A cat jumps across the shadow of a
minaret.

LILIES

1)   Dream: I'm going down the steps towards the Old
City. As I cautiously head over to the north side of town, I
feel some warmth at the back of my head. I move ahead
carefully, so I don't trample the flowers growing on every
step. The shells have gauged out the level surfaces of the
steps and with the rainwater, dirt has gathered in the
hollowed out cavities. I make sure to stand only at the edge
so I don't plunge into the abyss or squash the weak, pale
flowers, the sickly flowers.

2)   Which Fassbinder film was that in?
            A one-armed
            man
            goes into a florist and asks:
            which flower shows that the days are passing?

            And the florist says:
            white lilies

                            (Laurie Anderson)

CURFEW

After curfew, Tito Street is dead. Wind blows against the nylon windows. When it stops blowing, you can hear cats walking on the asphalt. Then, out of the dark, a man calls: "Who are you?" he asks. The narrow beam of his flashlight searches for my identity papers. One is meeting another— they signal to each other with their lights: the black helmeted driver of a Jeep without any windows, and a pick-up completely covered with iron panels—Dobrinja appears on it in yellow letters. When I turn into a narrow street, I think about how someone must be preparing to make a set like this for a science fiction film somewhere. An extra in that film is not as mortal as Sarajevo. Less real. I walked the main streets carefully, afraid that, in the dark, I might get tangled up in the fallen trolley wires. There aren't any on this street but, nevertheless, I keep on my toes. You can't see a thing but I know that, to my left, there is a kiosk. The glass is broken, the doors have been removed, and its insides have been cleaned out. The plucked shelves hang off the walls. From what was left, someone made a *precise* installation. On exhibit, behind no glass, a row of color photos of Sarajevo is hung on a string with clothespins. It's been that way for days already. The creator of this installation remains anonymous. It would be enough to simply reach in and take the postcards; it sure is strange that no one's tried yet.

GETTING THINNER

War is a time of crisis for the male gender. No one can convince me otherwise: war is spurred on by the *asexual*, the emotionally disturbed. Love offers deliverance from the *tyranny of the ego*: asexuality—combined with heavy political control—can only result in criminal perversity. I see young women change several times a day and, with make-up on, walk the empty streets of Sarajevo in which not even a single cafe is open. I know women who, in only two months, have lost so much weight so quickly, that they've also lost any sense of the erotic. And this too is a horrible result of the war: the Serbian leaders' tyranny of the ego reproduces itself in whatever space they make their presence known through war—they want to create an *asexual world*, no matter what the cost. I watch a famous actress hanging out with some young soldiers, defenders of the city. She's clearly having a good time and, every now and then, she delays her departure. Finally, though, they leave: the carefully chosen, refined words of the young defenders are exchanged for common jokes. Such consolation.

LOOTED STORES

1)   A young man in a black uniform walks through the display window of an abandoned store, his army boots graze the empty space, trampling thousands of pins that held men's shirts to cardboard backing, neatly packed in boxes. He sits at the register and taps at the keys with his fingers. He pulls out a laser gun and aims at the empty corners of the room, the red dot wanders across the wall and over the empty shelves. He puts the gun down on his knees and, still sitting, opens a drawer, takes out a comb, and carelessly runs it through his hair. Then he takes out a little porcelain figure of Jesus on the cross, with a wreath of thorns, and puts it on the table: his fingertips touch the porcelain figure cleanly. Bending over, he pulls a box with a shirt in it out from under his feet. The sole of a sneaker is still embedded on the chest of the unpacked shirt and his hand waves across the collar as if he were brushing it off. He pulls a pin out of the shirt and pounds it into the wooden edge of the table with the butt of his pistol. He puts the figurine of the crucified Christ on the shirt, right in the outline of the sole of the sneaker, before putting the box with everything in it on the table. He gets up: with the pistol dangling under his armpit, he goes outside combing himself.

2)   Maybe because of the war, just because of the war: it dawns on me that maybe factory packed shirts—with all the hundreds of little needles stuck in them—is just a marketing pitch aimed at the suffering of that marvelous young Jew.

IMAM BEY'S MOSQUE

1)   A girl opens the door to his house for me and I see him
unexpectedly—his hands busy around the stove—in a light
green sweater, smiling. The movement of his hand beckons
me to sit. I look at the row of videos by the television; my
first thought, curiously, is: could there, among all these
tapes, possibly be a film by Yilmaz Güney? And that very
instant, I give up asking him.

2)   Efendi Spahić (the Imam of the Bey's Mosque), had
three children and a grandchild that were killed by the shells
that fell on Dairam. Before that, his wife too; as if God had
taken her to Him, to protect her. So she wouldn't see. Here's
what I think: there are neither major nor minor tragedies.
Tragedies exist. Some can be described. There are others
for which every heart is too small. Those kind cannot fit in
the heart.

3)   I first saw this man on television: I trembled at the
abundance of spiritual power by which he gathered sorrow
into himself; he seems younger to me now, as he nears the
table, putting down a pack of cigarettes, holding an ashtray,
offering me one and saying: "I liked tobacco once, then I
stopped, and now I don't smoke anymore." He speaks softly.
When I speak softly, my voice becomes hoarse because of
the cigarettes. I stare at him attentively, searching for a sign
to reveal the power that distinguishes him. We speak; he
says: "People can be divided into the stronger and the

weaker, but you can't chastise the weak. There are reasons to justify their weakness: physical constitution, for instance. And a lot of other reasons. I could never slaughter a sacrificial lamb, a *kurban*, with my own hands, nor would I ever have the strength to do such a thing. So be it." Pointing out his own weakness, he shattered my naive conviction that signs of his strength could be seized at a glance.

4)   We speak; he doesn't improvise. His answers to the questions I pose have been thought out in advance. It seems that, in his solitude, he has thought through everything. That's why you feel a lightness as he speaks, his clasped fingers hugging his knees. His thinking is literary, visual. His answers are complete so that, gradually, the conversation unveils a small lexicon of the Imam's solitude.

Army. The Sarajevan soldiers are hunters, or so the story goes: like hunters, they go about their business all week and then, on Saturday, go into the woods and kill a rabbit before heading back home; that's how the soldiers are, or so the story goes — they sit in cafes and then hop into their fancy cars and head for the top of Bistrik, by Mount Trebević, to shoot.

Bosnian Muslim. I think of Tolstoy. He writes of Hadji Murad — awestruck by his rugged strength, and says: He's like grass in the fall, the hay carts pass over it, but when the wheels move on, every blade rights itself again. That's how the Bosnian Muslims are: blades of fall grass.

Mudjahadeen. The West has no idea what this means. In translation, it means "fighter." For them, he's a terrorist who throws bombs in Paris cafes. But he fights to fulfill divine justice; for him, killing in revenge is a capital sin. The West can't see this from its apathetic heart.

Islam. Faith in expansion, but without imposition; it has no missionaries. An I that doesn't pronounce itself, while leaving its abundant, human traces everywhere. And that is the trait of great people.

5)   I'm drawn to his measured way of speaking. All the questions I put to myself about this man have been betrayed. I call this, for myself and for lack of a better term, divine tolerance. As we pause — while Efendi Spahić gets up, pulls the door of the oven open and turns back with two pears on a tray — I take a look at the prints on the wall, one coppertint, all with motifs from Sarajevo's Old City. This is where I saw it, so that's why I'm appending it to the lexicon of our conversation here.

The Spirit of Sarajevo. Those Bosnian cafés come to mind: on the walls, the inevitable pictures with the same motifs: an old man with a fez holding a *findjan*; merchants gathered around a public fountain. There (in those cafés), pensioners in black berets with white packs of Drina cigarettes used to come by from their shops or from Friday prayers, and junkies used to come by, because of the cheap Coca-Cola. Sarajevo's tolerance, usually associated with the equilibrium of worshippers holding different faiths in the same narrow streets, it seems, just pronounces the naivete of historians. This is truly tolerance, and no one has written even one word about it: the equilibrium of Bosnian motifs in a picture on the wall with Coca-Cola; the same water boiling coffee for the old man in the beret and the long-hairs in jeans shooting up in the shadow of a minaret. This wasn't of importance to anyone. Historians haven't, for example, written anything about the Old City's tradition of naive art. I peel the pear: the conversation moves on to a more serene level: I distinguish yet another concept, and enter it into the lexicon.

Emir Kusturica. He is like a cow who has given a lot of milk and then, banging his foot into the pail, knocks it down and spills everything, says Efendi Spahić. When we part, I go out into the street calmer than when I had come. As Efendi Spahić spoke of his misfortune, his eyes—as if from cold—narrowed gently. Nothing more. I went out with the scent of fall pears in my nostrils.

6)   It's sunny, and the city is still enveloped in fog. Right at the bottom of the long, elegant steps to the Municipal Museum, Bokun sits: with his hair wrapped in a pony-tail, dark glasses and a black leather jacket, he looks like Michael Douglas's resigned double. Saturday: the weekend Chetniks are up on the hills: I tell him it's time we got off the street, but he waves his hand: "This is my last cigarette. It wants the respect it deserves. And I can only give it that on the street. It's only here that I'm alone enough," he says.

7)   I try to compare Bokun's solitude with the solitude of Efendi Spahić. I run out of breath walking uphill.

Reader, if you go up Abdullah Kaukji street another 50 meters, when you turn around you'll see Sarajevo in fog, a cosmos of sorrow; over the fog, you can see the rooftops of the Old City and right above, the minaret of the Bey's Mosque, isolated from the terrestrial, quotidian fog.

INNOCENT CIVILIANS

In front of the Theater—I almost bumped into her—a young woman pops out, spreading a cloud of perfume around her. Her tight skirt cuts her steps short. But this fantastic spectacle—like a spread in a fashion magazine—is only completed by a freshly bathed dalmatian trotting over the crushed cement and broken windows. He runs and weaves happily in her path over the shards of glass: she's beautiful, and the dog is beautiful. Don't they care about the war? They do, because shells are falling here: here, right where they are. Of course she's an innocent civilian, but not all civilians are innocent. There are those who, like retired couples, go out hand in hand for an evening walk in the middle of a war that they inspired, the course of its future in their heads. Of course, this business about civilians can get very complicated. You might run into a soldier pointing at the tip of his sneaker and the coagulated blood there that once belonged to a professor who thought that five thousand Muslim kids ought to be killed. Which means if civilians are innocent, soldiers are sinful and guilty. But soldiers, in a normal distribution of power, are just young people whose interests should be protected by some kind of youth movement. Of course nationalist-macho power cubed (power x power x power), holds generational interests beneath contempt since it conceives of things in millenial and mythological dimensions. As for feminism, that is, for women who—at least in light of this formula—are simply there to be demeaned, there's little use in war. In other words: just by looking at nationalist attitudes regarding generational and gender interests, you could see that war was inevitable. But you couldn't have foreseen that in such a short span of time, a young woman in front of the Theater could arouse the almost forgotten memory of a world in which something whole, beautiful and fragrant exists. Something like a silk scarf.

FIRES

After he finished taking pictures of the Library, Kemal Hadžić was wounded by a piece of shrapnel on his way home. It's hard to avoid a tendency towards mysticism during war: the first thing I thought of is that his wound was a warning. Kemal said that when he was wounded, he didn't feel any pain because of the shock. To feel the pain, you have to assume consciousness of it. And the state of shock, while it lasts, consitutes its own sojourn to *the other side*. At the same time, plunging into the world is its own art form: what else did this photographer do as he circled the burning library, looking for a perfect angle or enough light, catching the water of the Miljacka with a wide angle lens? What else if not to fulfill that passionate artistic desire of distilling wild beauty from the spectacle of death, of approaching it from the *other side*? The artist's need to venture into the *unknown* is risky, but it is precisely upon this impulse that the power of art is based. Maybe the shrapnel was a punishment for that heretical impulse. And maybe this is all smoke and mirrors, induced by my own fear of war or the boy in whom I recognize a being who doesn't belong to this reality. When Kemal was in shock, the boy followed him to the hospital and checked him in; then, after the doctors looked at him, the boy stayed to cool off Kemal's sweaty face with a rolled up newspaper. Because of that *angelic* gesture.

MILOMIR KOVAČEVIĆ

Ever since he's been a photographer, he's worn the same kind of iffy reddish-green sweater. He wore it in peace and Milomir Kovačević shot the entire war in Sarajevo in it. He managed to be wherever something was happening because he subjected everything to sight, even the body, for which one sweater is enough. Ambitious photographers are trying to show Sarajevo in ruins, as a place of death. From their pictures of the charred UNIS skyscraper, you can't see the former beauty of the city in the valley: students in shirtsleeves stroll by the university on a sunny day as snow on the peak of Mount Trebević reflects off the blue glass facade of the high-rise. Because the gaze has been so violently disrupted in this city, such photographs are descriptive, of no artistic merit. A photograph by Milomir Kovačević: with legs crossed—a boy? a girl? I'm not sure— a naked creature on the pavement sits in the lotus position. Nothing in the picture points to the war: the beatific smile and wire-rim glasses only make the similarity between this androgynous figure and Ghandi more apparent. Separated from the surrounding war, it would still be an interesting shot, a "moment of the world's totality." Yet, it is a war photograph that, paradoxically, is more accurate than those revealing the devastation of Marindvor. Everyone in Sarajevo, accustomed to death, lives through so many transcendental experiences that they have already become initiates of some deviant form of Buddhism. If the agression lasts another month or so, many of them will believe that a chestnut falling on Wilson's Promenade carries more weight than a grenade.

LION'S

The former municipal cemetary, brought back to life by the war. A trenchdigger shovels out new graves; he digs in advance, counting on dead bodies. When the shells fall—and they often fall on this cemetary—the trenchdigger's driver and the gravedigger helping him jump into the freshly dug graves. Forced trench: for an instant, something in death's domain serves life.

GLASS

1)   Standing by the window, I see the shattered glass of Yugobank. I could stand like this for hours. A blue, glassed-in facade. One floor above the window I am looking from, a professor of aesthetics comes out onto his balcony: running his fingers through his beard, he adjusts his glasses. I see his reflection in the blue facade of Yugobank, in the shattered glass that turns the scene into a live cubist painting on a sunny day.

2)   In the evening, I listen to the news along with the glazier, the Old City's master glass-man. At the mention of place names during dispatches from the battlefield, he appends his own lively anecdotes, the recollections of a man whose work took him all over Bosnia: here, he did the glass for a school; there, an auditorium or an arena . . . I listen to him like a student listening to a teacher. After the news, I experience Bosnia like a huge glass warehouse crackling through the thin wires of a transistor hooked up to a car battery. The homeland shatters brittlely in the ears of the glazier, her true president.

ZAMBAK / MUSLIMS

Many Muslims in Bosnia gave their children Eastern Orthodox names from what could be called a *partisan complex*. These poor kids were born into their parents' unnatural marriage to a state that delicately tried to assimilate them. It stands to reason, then, that a number of Muslim artists — when the war started — fled to Belgrade in military convoys. The very same convoys that brought the Chetniks to Sarajevo. They went to that very Belgrade from which the expulsion of Muslims on the Drina had been orchestrated. Many examples confirm this sense of inferiority. For instance, the coat of arms for the republic of Bosnia-Hercegovina is a flower. In Croatian, it's called *lijer* or *krin*. It's so stylized that it looks more like a cross than the flower which grows in Sarajevo's courtyards, that flower that's become so prominent lately, the lily. Consenting to the eastern version of the name isn't merely a way of getting by, but a rather stubborn confirmation of Yugoslavia. Bosnian Muslims needed a genocidal war to comprehend what Yugoslavia really means to them. It isn't simply a question of linguistic negligence. When a ten-year-old kid asks if he's a Muslim and after getting a positive answer says 'I don't want to be expelled,' then you know something horrible has happened to this people. Our language has sealed our fate. The kid asking — in a bomb shelter — sharpens his pencil with the jagged end of a piece of shrapnel and keeps on drawing his strip. He calls the hero of his comic Terry Marnes, he thought up the name himself. The world of the strip, as one level of the world's humanity and cultivation, doesn't exist at this moment. This kid's real world is the one he's found out about ten years too late: its borders begin and end at his name. The horrible thing that's happened to this people is oblivion, and the only thing worse than expulsion is losing the memory of expulsion.

KIDS

S: Harun, come on, get into the house, it's grenading outside.

HERO

He's a hero, says the soldier in fatigues, pointing at the kid kneeling on the parquet floor. Killed a Chetnik, he says. The boy put the ammunition belt and the old M48 down on the floor: he smiles, completely carried away, as he plays with plastic cars and makes the sounds of an engine. On Vraca, he says, after agreeing to tell the story, my friends took some shots with a kalashnikov and nothing. Then I let go twice and the Chetnik just rolled over. My rifle kills at ten miles, he said, scratching his forehead with a toy car.

GRENADE

Shells are constructed so shrapnel can't be cleaned out of the flesh, that's why there are so many amputations. Their power is a great stimulant to the soldier, that corpse in a trenchcoat, to his military autism. The utmost proclamation of existence is a soldier's signature on the casing of a shell. Europe and its "western sin" makes the end of the world imaginable, that need to affirm her own existence is also her curse. Graffiti scratched into bathroom walls: *this is my name, I exist,* and the grenades that leveled Sarajevo's maternity ward signed in oil: *this is me and by my being I will destroy other lives.* That's Europe, a sign of weakness: endless self-affirmation, the end of the world. Shells killing kids. Imaginations turned 180 degrees, gone wild, emptied of memory. This is probably sheer esoterica: I think about how their blocked consciousness is not a reaction to the images of war, but nature preparing them for long years of battle. What kind of curriculum will be put in place for kids ripped apart by shrapnel as sharp as razors? Imagine a teacher assigning "Snail House" or "The Enchanted Saddle." It's easier to think of war as their only school. And there are plenty of shells, they're so devastating that only the Schwartzeneggers have a chance to survive—at least acording to post-modern theorists—left to themselves, wandering naked through the global desert and the infosphere, new nomads freed from feudal prejudice, not as members of a nation but as carriers of information they'll exchange between themselves together in the planetary community. Right now it's true that shells are falling on Bosnia, in Sarajevo, but it's unlikely that's where it will end.

TRAFFIC

I pass through the shrouded streets, hidden from the gaze of snipers endowed with infrared rays that can pick me out in pitch darkness. At night, the red laser beam strays over the facades. I walk by feeling helpless, aware of the next second in which maybe I'll be, and maybe I won't. Like shadows, we're just passing through an illusion of the fourth dimension. Seen from our perspective, the transformation of city traffic ends Europe's indifferent view of the world, through which the Gordian knot can only be untied one way. Now I remember the paths beaten across yards that everyone uses instead of the pavement. One Sarajevo war-path leads through the ruins of a movie theater. Here, the ways part by themselves—not through urban planning or oblivious residents falling into line. *Don't put yourself on display*, that's the long and the short of pedestrian law, precisely the opposite of peacetime decrees: that is, stay on the main drag, and *be seen*. But the new paths don't have the finality of asphalt; they go through a metamorphosis to the same extent that shells alter the shape of the city. Constant unpredictability (maybe you'll be, maybe you won't), the constant pressures of new impressions make them (these paths), continually new. I've been seeing Nemanjina Street in a completely new light since yesterday: I saw ambulance beds with wheels on the pavement there, with grey leather covers. Pedestrians stretch out, roll their sleeves up over their elbows and wait for someone in jeans (under normal conditions, they'd be wearing white coats) to approach them with needles and clear plastic vials to draw their blood.

PHOTOGRAPHERS

1) December, the year 1991. Sitting around in the Theater Club, photographs by Mladen Pikulić on the wall (the show is called *Vukovar today . . . and tomorrow*?) The music is too loud; the crowd sits silently at their tables, pupils dilated. Overhead, waiters make their way through paths blocked by the dazed young bodies, huge stainless steel pitchers of draft beer and Coca-Cola in their outstretched palms. Bloody syringes lie on the floor in the toilet. And then, a young guy at one of the tables points to another young guy—the one in the picture crying before the background of Vukovar decimated by grenades—and says, in amazement: "He's got the same sweater on I got."

2) The photographers of Sarajevo—as opposed to their colleagues who come from abroad to collect their fees from dailies, weeklies and art magazines by trading in death— are the only chroniclers of war in this city; they run out of film and supplies and get no compensation for their work. This doesn't make them any different or their job more distinguished than that of surgeons, for instance, or firefighters. But their engagement is marked by an *intellectual morality*, something so rare in our parts both before and during the war. So a photographer made it possible for a junkie in a bar in Sarajevo to recognize his sweater on a guy in a picture from Vukovar. The grenades hadn't started falling here yet, but you could see—and how—that Sarajevo had already started wearing Vukovar's

[57]

sweater. Of this, the intellectuals — or at least those referred to as such — kept quiet.

The war didn't change anything; what, for instance, did writers do after the Library burned down? What about scholars and historians? Nothing. Maybe because they'd already stopped going there. But the Writer's Union, when their cafe was lost, they wrote endless protests and polemics in *Oslobodjenje*. The destroyed Library appeared on thousands of photographs . . . It became, among other things, part of the professional pathos: the Library in the foreground as a standard postcard of Sarajevo (chosen by photographers).

Maybe the guy in the picture wasn't even alive any more during Pikulić's "Eyewitness of War" exhibit. Today, I don't even know if the guy who pointed to the sweater in the picture is still alive either. The title of the exhibit extended itself to the question: *and tomorrow*? Everyone knew the answer to that was already contained in the question, but they hoped tomorrow wouldn't come.

I said everyone, but I am thinking first of the intellectuals who kept quiet, hiding in the promiscuous Sarajevo night, evading the moral obligation to at least say that leveling cities by grenade wasn't right. A photographer was one of the few who found himself among those who asked questions.

After ten months of war, you can still find "intellectuals" in Sarajevo asking: "Why is this happening to us, and why so brutally?" Fools, they don't see that the answer is: Because!

Just because.

And that's why it's too late now for any questions.

WOUNDED PARKS

1)   Goaded on by the fear of winter, residents of Sarajevo
have taken to cutting down trees in the city; if we don't
count the shelling, the predominant sound in town is the
buzz of chain saws. Ordinary scenes: men pull a cable
wrapped around a poplar toward themselves as it rests
before swaying to the left and right as kids run around
cheering, some for the men and some for the tree, and when
it falls a view of the woods on Mount Trebević bursts open;
an unusually tall man, his hair grey and well-groomed,
wearing a sharp new suit, a bow-tie and shiny shoes, carries
an attache case in his left hand while with his right he drags
an enormous chestnut bough chopped down in the park
through the door to the lobby of his building.

2)   "A full-fledged attack is being carried out against our
urban greenery. Trees are being cut down in our parks, along
the streets and even in cemetaries. We call upon all citizens
to preserve our urban greenery. Those who disobey this
appeal will be severely punished."
    The only conclusion I can reach from this text, published
in a Sarajevo daily, is that if I don't protect the urban
greenery—being busy with my own work—I'll be
punished severely. Neverthless, on the north side of town
you can hear the mournful wailing of chain saws: people in
the city are desperate, like anyone thinned out before the
coming of winter.

WAR PROFITEERS

We've begun to distance ourselves from those "social structures" that—during the first days of the war—allowed someone, with no sense of guilt or shame, to walk into a construction site, haul ceramic tiles out of an unfinished building, and simply walk off with them. A middle-aged guy could walk down the longest avenue in Dobrinja: on his shoulder, he'd have a box of ceramic tiles; with his right hand, he drags a long iron rod along the asphalt creating such unbearable noise that passersby just stop to stare at the carefree thief in amazement. Taking his sweet time, he'd move on with his plunder as a kid shuffled along after him. Amongst those not considering, or at least not thinking past the "Eternal Now," are the four guys who pulled a truck up to Yugoplastika: two stood guard with revolvers while the other two methodically cleaned the place out, neatly placing school supplies and raincoats under a tarp on the back of the truck. Anyone displaying the slightest sign of protest, got a quick warning as shots fired into the air. Thanks to the lack of any control over weapons, in besieged Sarajevo the phenomenon of stolen cars simply got out of hand. Between the snipers' bullets and the shelling, limousines became completely expendable, like paper towels. A more serious instance of war profiteering could be witnessed the day the city was inundated with Bordeaux two-door compacts. Someone had pulled a whole bunch of them out of storage, and the streets were filled with them. While the petty war profiteers were dealing unbottled beer, loaded into canisters that smelled like kerosene—so that by noon the stupified bodies of men and women lay by the empty containers—the more influential crooks dealt in the bodies of those willing to pay plenty for a way out of the besieged city.

WHITE DEATH

When snow falls on Sarajevo, when pines crackle with frost, the bones underground will be warmer than us. People will freeze to death: a winter without fire is coming, a summer without sun has past. The nights are already cold and when someone's dog starts barking on a balcony, a chorus of strays answers back, howling in sorrow like children crying: even Irish setters, usually so filled with glee, bark sadly at night in this town, like Ruthger Hauer in the last scene of *Blade Runner*. Snow will bury this city just the way war has buried time: what's today? When is Saturday? The daily rituals are dead, just like the yearly ones. Who, in December, will print a calender for 1993? There is night, there is day: in them are people prepared for the end of the world, well aware that existence in its plenitude would be all but lost were they unconscious of global cataclysm. That's why they burn a small light at the first sign of dark: the wick pulled through a ball-point refill, a cork wrapped in tinfoil to keep the oil in the lamp made out of an empty beer can burning on the surface. And in the small, clear blaze they can see that intimate objects and faces have an earthly glow, and that there is no grief, until *aksham* falls, at the sunset call for prayer.

POLITICS

We're talking. A., right between a falling shell and what he was talking about, stops mid-sentence and says: *there*, as if the grenade confirmed the truth of his thoughts.

Journalists describe this *there* every which way in their writing, but no one uses it as deliberately as politicians.

Substantiating every opinion, *there* assumes the shelling — and death is just icing on the cake. Death confirms a thing can be true only if blood is dripping from it.

The most political phrase that's come up during these years goes like this: The war in Sarajevo isn't horrible *because you can hear it*. This was uttered with such indifference, you can be sure the guy who said it got out of town soon after saying it.

It would be true (that phrase) when the weight of one tragedy could erase another; that is, when tragedies could be comparable. It is precisely upon phrases like this that political gains are consolidated.

VESTIBULE

From some naive belief that this is the way to defend our homes, we keep watch in the vestibule night and day. When the wind blows through the open doors, the toppled figures on the chessboard tremble easily as you hear the soft touch of wood against wood. In front of the vesitibule, we've constructed a bunker out of densely piled cement blocks. At the hour our heads turn to the transistor and we stare at the broken digital clock on the radio, at the red, pulsing zero. What do the reporters say? The wind blows and a sniper's bullets whiz by the entrance. A wet, April snow is falling. The vestibule lights up at night only when you open the door to the elevator. A woman brings coffee down, served on the metal trays we used to use for grilled meat. The polish on her nails has chipped. After the morning shift, I go up to the roof of the building: it's still dark. Leaning on the elevator shaft, I sit on the wide gas pipes, beautifully wrapped in shiny aluminum foil. I light up a cigarette and look at the tanks on Mojmilo. They're level with my line of vision so I can hear the soldiers breathing as they take their morning workout. The orders are less audible than their breathing. Dark silhouettes against the violet tint of the sky, you can make out the soldiers' athletic shirts in the darkness. A sharp wind blows off the moss, smacking the Yugoslav flag against the flagpole. I look on with great interest. I remember my first morning in the Yugoslav National Army, when I was taken into the mess hall. It was cold and dark, just like this. The whole place reverberated with an eerie sound I'll remember for the rest of my life: soldiers hitting sticks of butter with the handles of their knives, to defrost it. And the same feelings come back to me.

WHAT WILL YOU REMEMBER?

I remember a conversation from ten years ago. It was snowing and a kid asked me: What's the most important thing in life? I said something, even though I didn't have an answer to his question. The kid, however, didn't even listen but answered it himself with more than some conviction: I think the most important thing in life is for a lot of things to happen to you, so you'll have something to remember!

When something is articulated with such simplicity, you can always recognize the truth of it. Besides my encounter with the boy, I also remember the bright lights of the busy, wide streets in Dobrinja.

During the war, when I got to the center of town from Dobrinja, I was sorry that I hadn't brought my scrapbooks with me, even though they were filled with snapshots that only preserved all the more or less insignificant data of my life. But without them, it was as if proof of my past had been wiped out. As if every moment I lived had been in vain.

This is a feeling of absolute sorrow, along with the consciousness of ultimate loss. It's the same feeling I recognized in the final scene of *Blade Runner*: naked, the last android is dying in the rain—and that's the instant that the body, in which not a single feeling had dwelt until then—is filled with sorrow at the realization it is the last of its kind. The android remembers experiences lived through and, because of this, gives his life to the hunter, his sworn enemy but the only one who can preserve any memory of him.

I never had the urge to break a secret: I wouldn't ask a

technician to explain what the reason was for discolored photos, like when the eyes of everyone in a shot come out red. It never occurs to me to ask for the reason, because I want to maintain my faith in the secret power whose only way of showing itself is by hiding behind the red eyes of a photograph.

I often recognize people who aren't alive any more in war photos that I see. They were here and now they aren't. That means, amongst other things, that the war has also gotten old. Thousands of false divisions have been made up in Sarajevo. But the only one that matters is between the living and the dead since that, essentially, is how the world divides itself. As far as war photographs go, I don't really know what purpose they serve, other than the everyday needs of newspapers and magazines. They're useful only given the assumption that you'll survive: what other reason could there be, if you can't even remember your red eyes in the picture?

The war has shown you can't even rely on someone else's memory.

In Sarajevo, it only makes sense to remember the day that's just passed. It's snowing, like it's supposed to in January. I'm watching kids sledding. They can be divided up into those who are in love with their sleds and those who just love sledding—the sleds serve them, and it seems like they're barely even aware of how they look. I saw this today and I'm very happy as I write about my discovery. I know that, when everything passes, I'll remember this too . . .

RUINS

I know most of the people passing in the street. The circle is getting smaller. Once I used to think *solitude* meant there was someone in this city, a man or a woman, whom I'd never meet. The city is receding. We step over shards of glass on the street; cars without even one window left slow down and carefully drive over smoldering trolley cables. The shells that came down on the National Bank have created a distinct stone relief on its facade: reality is recognized in its wholeness only as it shatters to bits. The glass on the street is less an example of "a shattered image of reality" than the wide, light-brown bands of packing tape that "whole" panes of glass are held together with in Sarajevo. The common sense of tenants whose only thought is that things get no worse than they are — this is the consciousness of disappearance. Nothing has remained whole, not even the whole panes of glass held together by tape. The people I meet don't talk about what was — everyone is besieged by what is *now*; person — torso. The unity of time has been broken. That awful smokers' habit hasn't even survived — to lick the length of a cigarette and make it last longer just evokes this poverty that is the present. Every day you hear about someone you know who was killed. Here's where we played pool before the war: such idleness could only lead to no good. Someone no longer here went out that door and ran through the streets, his hands smeared in blue chalk. My son clipped an obituary from the paper, glued it to an $8^1/2$ x 11" sheet and below the photo of the dead soldier wrote: *this guy I knew I met him in a restaurant*. What remains bare disappearance in the newspaper becomes the consciousness of disappearance in a child's gesture.

S., in front of the mirror: she's happy with the weight she's lost during the war. Those with definite plans about the future of their bodies survive.

WAR

War
and nothing is going on —
I go into town to beg for cigarettes

I've always known your scent
but you've never been closer —
sometimes when it's cold in the morning you
put my underwear on by mistake

in ten years we haven't been together as much
as we have these five months —
now you've got my sweater on all day

your joy
at the packets of humanitarian aid
makes me happy and sad at the same time

and I ask myself: where on earth do
you find us coffee every night?

There isn't a single pane of glass left in our windows
and there's just no way to get rid
of the lagging flies

ANIMALS

I'm beginning to enjoy all this. There's enough danger, and plenty of sorrow. I'm lying down and I can't help thinking: how long can this kind of life go on? The cat sleeps on my chest. She is chosen: over the glint in her eyes is a mark in the shape of an M. I didn't know: you told me that day I went wild and wanted to crush her, to crush her cat nature. Then you revealed the pattern on her forehead and said:

"Only cats touched by Muhammad have an M."

Since then I've let her do whatever she wants, sleep wherever she happens to be. I don't know how long this kind of life can go on. I get a thrill every time the cat snaps out of her slumber at the din outside and I feel the slow unsheathing of her claws on my chest.

CAT

What's changed? I've come to have faith in the non-human. And not just that: I already assume everything else to be human, that is, no good. It's already a year that I've been learning from cats, from their fluidity, from the self-satisfaction of this singularly fluent form. People only like animals in whom they recognize human characteristics. That's why they like dogs, because canines show their happiness and sadness the same way, maybe even more transparently, with their big, moist eyes. Animals have developed into a Western cult, and the ability to communicate between two conflicting worlds (the human and the non-human), has been codified into fairy tales. Alan Parker made a film in which he implanted human characteristics into the body of a canary. In one of the horror scenes with creaking doors, a reddish cat suddenly assaults the bird. The cat is evil incarnate, simply because human characteristics cannot be implanted into its body. Those characteristics that we connect to the so-called "soul."

In the Western mythology of Disneyland, cats merit the least sympathy. Mice, as the victims of cats, according to the tendentious logic of American fairy tales, are superior beings who deserve more sympathy. Of course this is related to the fact that the status of victim must remain an exclusively human category (and this relationship of victim and victimizer is not without religious origins). Anyone thinking rationally would have to agree it's a mean feat to attribute cleanliness to these creatures of the cellar, producers of fevers, plagues, and a whole range of diseases that lead to truly horrifying forms of death. For such an animal to become an object of sympathy seems absurd. On the other hand, cats who groom themselves like hygienic dynamos, not only come out on top when it comes to mice but are so self-sufficient that they're not dependent on people. It's simply unnecessary for them to emulate human characteristics in order to gain some sympathy from a superior earthly being whose every utterance begins with the word "I".

This is not to say that feline characteristics can't be recognized in human behavior. Human gestures not administered by the soul can be thought of as feline. The human activity that presumes emotional withdrawal in the service of other interests is called politics. A cat, for instance, will stay on with a family of humans only under the condition that everything can be geared to its own advantage. If things are otherwise, the cat will go out in search of a new home. You could say that a cat is, literally, a political animal.

SHELTER

I'm running across an intersection to avoid the bullet of a sniper from the hill when I walk straight into some photographers: they're doing their job, in deep cover. If a bullet hit me they'd get a shot worth so much more than my life that I'm not even sure whom to hate: the Chetnik sniper or these monkeys with Nikons. For the Chetniks I'm just a simple target but these others only confirm my utter helplessness and even want to take advantage of it. In Sarajevo, death is a job for all of them. Life has been narrowed down completely, reduced to gestures. It's almost touching to see the comic motion of a man covering his head with a newspaper as he runs across this same street, scared of a sniper's bullet.

Bernard-Henri Lévy has described the war in Sarajevo as a classic *medieval siege*. True, except that nowadays the means of killing are somewhat more destructive. Being in this city means you have no cover, you're in mortal danger every second of the time. The sense of helplessness comes from having your own body occupy the space of your mortality, and the constant shelling doesn't let you stop thinking about it. To survive mentally, you need to find the most soothing shelter possible. Experience has shown that the most effective means of shelter is made of books. In our neighborhood, a shell hit a storage bin for bottled gas; hissing, the gas inundated the whole street with a ghastly smell. This, according to the experts, was quite dangerous, so the next day we filled every little opening with books.

There were a lot of them around since we emptied the fallout shelter which was used before the war as a warehouse for the municipal library. When a shell falls, books act like a net, trapping the shrapnel within them. A guy I know had his life saved because his wife worked in a Marxist library where she used to keep getting free copies of Lenin, Engels and Kardelj.

A typical Kafkaesque metaphor—the *book covers your head* —has become real for us. A poet in Sarajevo built a real bunker out of books. He put a thick book with a deluxe, vinyl cover by the window at the entrance, like a lookout party facing the front line: *With Tito To Victory*. Quite an odd choice for *scripture that shields the poet's dwelling.* I have my own scripture: a friend of mine gave me a copy of a fax with a stylized sabre and rifle on it, framed in Arabic script. The fact is I thought scripure was written by hand and that it served to protect as a *living manuscript.*

Like this, a fax mediates between me and God, and I believe I'm covered.

WASHING THE DEAD

The city's wasted and cut in half. Very few cars drive by the barracks. You have to be one hell of a driver to dodge the obstacles on the road, especially at the speed you have to travel in order not to get hit. I'm more than a bit reluctant, since I have to drive by the barracks every day. Even though, I must admit, there's something very cool about driving through an empty city that I just can't explain.

Every morning, there's a woman on Malta hitching a ride. When I'm on the road, I get the feeling that I'm the last person left alive in the city. So I stop for her happily, with the feeling that I can divide the risks of driving by two.

Hajra works in the baths, she bathes the dead. For every dead man she says: Nice! And for every woman, Nice! For some, she says: Nice, nice, nice! I washed him with hot water . . .

When she says that it makes a difference if the dead have been washed with hot or cold water, you get the feeling you should believe her . . . Hajra is so close to death, you could almost say death is her employer.

In some superstitious way, I have the feeling that death is a little more indulgent toward me around the barracks, a little more lenient with me since every morning I give this cheerful woman, death's own employee, a ride. I figure that all my automotive favors shouldn't be underestimated. Like the mythical boatman, I had my car—and I often picked the dead up from the street and brought them in to the clinic. Hajra called these my good deeds.

I discovered a number of things like this. For instance, I found that death is repetitious. At the intersection by the Twin I picked up an old man who died at the clinic. Two months later, I picked a young guy up from the same spot. In both cases, I was met by the same medical team: both of them were put in the same room, in the same bed. The symmetry is complete when I add that they were father and son.

Nothing about death can be said with sorrowful phrases.

When my neighbor's father died, we buried him in the cemetery by the Emperor's Mosque. Then the shells started raining down at the burial. I noticed something. The believers didn't panic: they calmly found cover on the veranda and under the eaves of the entrance to the mosque. Those who didn't speak to Allah in the familiar, wildly piled into their cars and fled down the empty streets. My neighbor as well. For days I tried to convince him to ride over to his father's grave with me, since he didn't stay through the burial. But he keeps refusing, justifying it through his fear of passing the barracks.

Regarding death, Hajra only really got to me this morning. As soon as she got into the car, she made sure to give me a gift immediately. Soap and a towel. I leaned over to accept her gift but she told me not to make such a big deal over it, she had plenty more where that came from. Of that, I had no doubt. Just as I stopped thanking her, she said:

I set it aside just for you . . .

The rest of the day I couldn't get my mind off the soap and towel set aside just for me in the trunk of my car. As time passes, I'm beginning to warm up to the idea more and more, me, a dead man, bathing himself in hot water.

EXODUS

Besides the tragic migrations that the media expediently uses the racist term "ethnic cleansing" to describe, other, less tragic migrations also exist: people leave one part of town for another, seeking cover in "less threatened areas," in quieter neighborhoods. This, supposedly, isn't evacuation but simply a temporary movement of people and objects. An old man guarding over at the Worker's College warns anyone who decides to go by there that they can't pass: "The Vijećnica is over there," he says, pointing at piles of books in the hallway, taken into hiding here from the burned out library. With every new migration, another superfluous burden of paper is thrown out. Political parties move, chucking archives, books, and photographs of Josip Broz into containers—after such cleansing, you'll need a candle to find a photograph with the Marshall on it. Socialism is thrown out on the street, just like outdated Yugoslav dinars: the wind blows them across the pavement. And among the refuse, you could also find—at least for the Liberals— overly ideological baggage like the following report:

Number: 6705/47; Sarajevo, 19. XI. 1947. year.: Yugoslav Communist Party Local Committee, Mostar;—Call Mida Čadro in and inform her that the CP is of the opinion that she must cut off all intimate relations with Tom Vikić, since the aforementioned has a wife and three children and the CP cannot agree to him divorcing his wife, meaning that a marriage between herself and Vikić will not come to pass; CP organizational instructional unit ; (signature illegible).

BERNARD-HENRI LÉVY

In front of the TV cameras, just as he's speaking to a reporter, Bernard-Henri Lévy is forced to lie down properly and find cover as the bullets whiz by. Sitting on the sidewalk, he continues speaking. Lévy in Sarajevo talks about what is happening in Sarajevo. Images of this interview will go around the world: he saw it all, there can be no illusions, he knows exactly what is going on here—his words inform Europe. This city could be liberated tomorrow, according to him, at least. He was one of the first to point out the horrors of the Gulag to his own people, blind to the evil of death camps. To take a stand, that is the duty of an intellectual in this century, wrote Lévy, the engaged intellectual, in his edifying and informative work. In front of the camera, not without some satisfaction, he speaks as the bullets fly by. There is a perverse sense of pleasure in this for a thinker whose positions are confirmed at the very moment he announces them to the world. Lévy's engagement becomes a tool of television—he is participating in the war, everyone can see that now. The magnificent narcissism of a thinker who, actually, can't inform a world blind for truth of anything—all he can do with his words and appearance is give the mass media monster a little help in turning war into the simulation of war.

The relationship of Europe and the world to our tribulations reminds me of an African soldier from UNPROFOR as she tried some yellow tights on, indifferent to the stares of everyone in the marketplace.

LAPIŠNICA / EDUARD LIMONOR

Lapišnica is a hill overlooking the Old City of Sarajevo; actually, it's a slope whose existence, at least by that name, only a few people in town knew about. Now everyone knows, and they say: That's Lapišnica, since it's the first place the Chetniks began shelling the city from. Eduard Limonov is a Russian emigré, an avant-garde writer. His literary work, which certainly commands critical respect, consists of novels that privilege the position of the outsider envious of physical power and—to make things perfectly clear—prepared to demonstrate this envy at a moment's notice. Why has Limonov come to Pale to inspire the Chetniks? Certainly not because of sweet old time religion. He comes to Pale, primarily, for literary consistency. *Serbia among the plums* is also an outsider, unrecognized, subject to economic sanctions since everyone suddenly began to meddle in her fascist affairs. She shows such undeniable strength through shelling, bombing, missiles, and chemical weapons, but you never know, so now the school of surrealushes needs inspiration. That's why Eduard Limonov (Edička, the hero of his novels) has made the pilgrimmage to Lapišnica so that, from this already consecrated slope, he can spit on Sarajevo, a hick town somewhere in the vicinity of Pale.

SIGN

Before I go on, I just want to say: an apartment burned down in Dobrinja. Everything in those rooms went up in flames, everything except a pastel in a carved wooden frame. That pastel with an almost plastic tear drawn on a child's face. This same motif was sold big time in front of the cathedral before the war.

Everything the Chinaman sold, he sold big time. He made aluminum *findjans* and covered them in enamel to simulate copper. When he did a job, he'd go into a cafe and line all his rage up along the bar. Then he'd tell the bartender:

Follow me! He'd take him to the toilet and carefully watch as every bottle of alcohol was emptied. He'd pay for everything, then spend the rest of the night at the bar, keeping only a bottle of whiskey at his side.

The Chinaman chose the night of his ritual carefully. It would always be when you could see a full moon in the sky. That was the night of his fear. To expel his own demons, he'd make a spectacle out if it.

The most important thing in life is to cut, he used to say back when he was selling those pastels with the plastic tear by the cathedral. He bought the carved wood by the yard, custom made for him by a carpenter someplace in a Serbian village. When it came, his workers would cut all night. Women passing by the cathedral would usually wave to him; once a woman said:

I won't have tears in my house!

Such commercial pressure was a challenge to the devil.

The Chinaman brought tears into his customers' houses, and took their money in exchange. No one is surprised anymore by the way people carry on when the moon is full. No one.

The tear in the boy's clear eye is a sign of the devil. People quickly forget evil because they still haven't created a language to describe it so the world refuses to carry the burden, preferring to forget.

That's why the devil appears openly in recognizable signs: horns and a tail are appended to a human figure. Right by fields full of wild sunflowers, the machinery of mass murder functioned smoothly in Hitler's camps. Who remembers the tyranny of death? Who feels its pain?

Hitler is easy to draw, any kid can do it. All you have to do is make a circle for his head and add the mustache. With the passing of time, even Hitler has been turned into an innocuous sign.

MASSACRE

Shots of the mass killing at Ferhadija circle the globe; pictures of the dead and massacred turn into an ad for the war. It doesn't matter that these people have names: TV translates them into its cool language, the naked image. The camera disembowels images of their psychological content to create information. And all the massacres that follow reproduce these same images. So the world can see what is going on here. But is this really possible when television sees right through the lack of compassion in human nature, just as long as tragedy doesn't hit home? The sense of tragedy arrived with the body bags wrapped in the American flag, and not before then, not through TV reports from Vietnam. Massacres happen to us, we empathize with our own tragedies. It's as simple as that. Maybe it's meager consolation, but the nature of the media is more realized for us: we see through it like the inner workings of a car on an exploded diagram, without detaining ourselves on the violet glow of the monitor. Everything else is window-dressing: the CNN cameraman, unbelievably new and undamaged equipment at his side, looks down a devasted alley on Bistrik. There's no one left on the deserted street, just flame shooting out of a burning drugstore.

FREEDOM

First of all I want to say the following: for over a year already, as long as the war has been going on, I've been writing about my experiences in Sarajevo. I don't even dare think about anything beyond this city—everything that isn't part of my own personal experience, is simply guesswork. Those with no faith in themselves keep on speculating, while the world maintaining this siege has nothing but contempt for them.

Writing only about things that I actually saw with my very own eyes, I was subjected neither to censorship nor self-censorship. It simply didn't exist. Such freedom, for someone engaged in this kind of work, is entirely adequate. On the other hand, I didn't see the effect of writing, in any form, during the war. But that would be a futile task, given the extraordinary need for people to read.

At the market I saw a counter with a newspaper on it accompanied by a sign saying: one reading, two cigarettes! With more than some curiousity, I stood off to the side, just to see if anyone would take up the offer. Before I knew it, a young guy with a beer bottle in his pocket came up to the counter and "bought a reading."

In Sarajevo, all published sources of information are referred to as "the press." But no one, for instance, calls books "the press." And reading the press has become a vice here, like cigarettes or alcohol. People still read, and listen to the news on transistors, following reports about peace.

It's very difficult to live with the perpetual expectation of better days to come, as you witness each month getting harder than the last. What do we do? We wait for Bosnia to get better. For fifteen months radio, TV and the newspapers promise peace. But the desired direction in which the course of the war is to be carried out isn't even known. For those whose job this is have yet to define either any strategic or political objectives. Days and months pass hopelessly waiting for peace or freedom, even though the meaning of these words have been completely obscured.

During the war I've experienced moments that had the taste of freedom, without this being a paradox. I was "happy" then "because I was conscious of myself without being afraid" (Benjamin). Freedom during war doesn't mean freedom of the individual, with its metaphysical dimension: it can even be experienced in a camp. In war, its meaning is bound to the collective, making peace and freedom the same.

The collective is a mob that suffers in silence, and waits. That's how it is in Sarajevo. That's how it was when the trollies ran: when the power was cut, people simply got out without asking for their money back; others got in, neatly destroyed their tickets and patiently waited for hours until the power came back on and the trolley started moving again.

In mythological time, the man engaged, someone who "thinks their own reality," recognizes "charisma" by his very deeds. Such a person believes that his influence on the course of events is decisive: he names streets and nations, making sure his words reach the ears of those who can turn his ideas into action. On his missionary journey, he can already count, right from the start, on the glory of the person who first said this or that. He wants to get paid for his ideas. These dreams are not grotesque: the fact that they have already been associated with a belief in the existence of people who can bring such ideas to realization means that individuals as such actually don't exist.

Walter Benjamin writes of a conversation with Brecht in which he articulated a critique of fascism. He was left with the impression of a man who "emanates the power of a grown-up in order to confront the power of fascism," a power that emerges from the depth of history, a place no shallower than where the forces of fascism originate. That was an illusion. But we live in times when even such an illusion is no longer possible, since the world remains bereft of great individuals. This is certainly the case in politics. No one who can offer the world a vision of salvation, nor are there people who could carry out the realization of such an illusion.

War is mythological time. The world is polarized and opposites have become that much more apparent. And everything is clean, like in a child's world. A child says: it's cold as heaven, probably since he's heard people say it's hot as hell so many times. In my search for moral consolation, as infantile as I knew that was, I thought up the following distinction: to be in Sarajevo means being in the world of truth. Out of town, where fascism rages, people dwell in a world of lies. Infantile indeed.

These days, I pass through streets famous for massacres:

in a passageway I see a display case with an advertisement for photographs. In one picture, four skydivers create the figure of a dancer in the air. They smile, overwhelmed by a feeling of freedom, conscious of the fact that they're flying. But there is nothing angelic in this spectacle: their smiles are almost hysterical, maybe because of the packs on their backs that skydivers still have to reconcile themselves with. More proof that every form of freedom is inevitably connected to risk. And even though their faces are clearly different, their individual fate is wiped out by the signature beneath the photo: *Produkt von Kodak*. What remains, then, is an ad for the photo itself, for the incomparable quality of its color. And this informs an age in which advertising has definitively replaced criticism.

A constant discomfort derives from this—writing these sentences, or any other for that matter—I am writing an ad for the war.

With that, every utterance about freedom finishes.

SURPLUS HISTORY

A shell hit one of the facades on Marshall Tito Street. The plaster poured down and, with it, a sheet metal sign. The sign read: Dr. Ante Pavelić 11. Until then I had no idea, but now I knew: the central street of Sarajevo had a different name fifty years ago, and that name was hidden for years behind the plaster, like in a geological diagram of different ages.

Time moves at such a clip these days that I get the feeling anything I look at or encounter here is older than I am. That includes every subject whose year of production predates the war.

Yesterday I was watching a movie shot in Sarajevo and I saw Marshall Tito Street in winter, prettied up for the New Year. From the Café Park to the Eternal Flame seemed like an immense space, a hazy abyss filled with makeshift counters piled up with balloons and greeting cards. Thousands of cars raced in either direction, and behind them a thicket of posters and lanterns. That scene made me realize I had completely forgotten how this street once looked, a street that now I seemed to be able to cross in just a few minutes. It was once so big I never would have considered walking the length of it; I'd always catch a trolley or take a cab.

The city has flattened itself out, like a military map.

Of course, it always took the same number of steps to go from the Café Park to the Eternal Flame. What's actually changed? That once this was called Ante Pavelić Street and now Marshall Tito Street is merely ideological trimming: parallel to this street, regardless, the same Miljacka flows.

I'm the one who's changed. Disabused of certain notions of comfort, we experience everything more normally. People died then too, only death is more stripped down these days: the lore accompanying death is a lot less eerie. The wrapping on the carton from which I've just taken a cigarette is actually documentary material. Because of the paper shortage, the tobacco factory uses any leftover materials they can find: the wrapping might be toilet paper or even pages from a book so that in the leisure time tobacco affords you can read fragments of a poem or the ingredients of a bar of soap. Foreigners buy cigarettes here as souvenirs, to bring home as living proof of this new tobacco art.

The cigarette I am smoking now was wrapped in a paper confirming someone's death: the cause of death is written on it, and you can see the signature and official stamp of the physician. I admit that this is the last piece of paper a cigarette should be wrapped in; at the same time, I must admit there isn't much left that can shock me.

The gap between the existence of a sign inscribed with the name Dr. Ante Pavelić Street and the signs now adorning the facades of Sarajevo's main drag, is filled with papers diagnosing death. It's called history. I've long ago lost the sense that words like history and progress have meanings that might ever coincide. Progress definitely doesn't exist in that sense, and we live in a space infected by a surplus of history. And when that's how it is, it's only natural for history to serve someone's interests. Down to the very last puff.

NEW EXPERIENCE

War is a word that I pronounced very easily not too long ago: now it's filled with the weight of true meaning. Life itself has revealed this, as simply as when you draw some water in from a channel in the river and find a corpse.

Now I'm learning things all over again. This May I found out what the word abundance means. There were so many cherries in the grass under the treetops that I walked around freely, only picking the nice, juicy ones. The possibility to choose, this is abundance.

In my thirty third year, I am owning up to my first experience. I walk along the street and look into the face of someone passing. At first, I look for signs of the proximity of death. Then I notice that smiles are disfiguring. A real face is much more beautiful without a grimace, no matter what kind of joy produces it.

I used to harbor doubts as to the existence of history. My consciousness of time was so fantastic that I couldn't possibly imagine my father was alive before I was born: his existence could only be dated from my first memory of it. This morning, I compared my palm with my son's palm: the lines embedded in our skin are of the same depth. In terms of suffering, my son and I are twins.

There is no more trustworthy measure of time. Every change confirms the superfluousness of people in the world.

The here and now exists. I seldom wake up with a dream I can remember; when I do, I dream about the war. S. dreamt that she was on Marshall Tito Street. It was so quiet you could hear the flight of flies through the air. She was alone on a street expecting the arrival of a convoy. Then she noticed someone leaning on a gutter. He had his back to her and when she approached him, his face turned out to be that of a young man of indeterminable age ("He could have been twenty, or thirty-five," she said). His straight black, Indian hair outlined the porcelain hue of his skin: when he smiled, his teeth were brilliantly white.

What are you doing here? she asks.

I'm waiting for the convoy, he says. My name's Mongrel and I have to get out of here, he says, 'cause there's no place for me here.

TUNNEL

A winter night without frost
but the cat fell asleep with the dog —
In the Bugatti Café
a pair of lovers
are so enthralled
by each other's caress
that their coffee just sits
cold and untouched —
It is they who trade heat
since the young are tactile —
probably less than 35 between them
but everything points to
plans they've dreamt up just half
an hour before curfew —

Just then in an instant no
different than any other
the crystal of a Rolex gleams
at the door of the Café Bugatti —
The guy with the watch is the Chinaman
and he takes a head count of the patrons
with the arrogance of a star
since it's true that a legendary thief
has to be a man of the world and
just because of that he looks the way
he does with a tail like Karl Lagerfeld —

What is there for someone like that
to see in the Café Bugatti
half an hour before curfew?
What follows is
a story of snow melting
the weight of human endeavor
and the severity of a world in which
every passionate desire is fulfilled
so late it turns into punishment —
To be without need
hushed to the likeliness death exists —
He's never got a fixed plan
but with his gift of improvisation
the Chinaman already seduces the kid
without ever letting the girl in on it —

That's how you gain the trust of a man
who sees a guy with a Rolex in front of him —
He promised a way out of the city
with such ease that even
the girl begins to believe it
and rightly so
because what the higher-ups can't do
a crook in good standing damn well can
10 minutes before curfew —

And as the Bugatti closes
the time has come to pay a visit
to the Chinamen's 1500 square feet

all laid out in parquet —
When the French cognac opens
the boss calls it heat —
All right already if you're
impatient just fill out the forms
but neatly legible like
bureaucracy is merciless —
You've got to be calm tonight
because only the tranquil inherit
the world out there surely whoever
made up the forms knew that —
An almost animal desire is all that can
take every part of your soul through the tunnel
to the south of the city
a tunnel in which water drips between the cables
and a living body gets to know
what it's like to be six-feet under —

A quarter of the bottle serves as measure
and the Chinaman knows the perfect moment
for the drama's turning point —
Pretending to be drunk
he begins to lay out a whole field of freedom —
L'Occident is scary enough, you
know naive, romantic lovers never make it
before they put the final touch on solipsism —
Ah, 4 times
the Chinaman uttered *solipsism*
convinced these kids

didn't know the meaning of the word —
and that's really the truth
since he'd already converted
it for them into his own
Chinese —
The lovers were ready for anything
when
the girl noticed his canine
and the diamond engraved in his tooth —
Make love in front of the Chinaman? All right

and she strips
but that isn't enough
to get by out there —
So the last twist comes
the final fatal tactic
and now a cobra
stands erect on a woman's body
tattooed over the Chinaman's broad chest
in the rainy night —
Snow is melting in the world
and love turns to punishment
for those who shoulder the world's
rage sullen and naked in their solipsism
The woman's frightened eyes
evade the young man's crazed look —
Her lips say *I love you*
before her eyes shut completely
abandoning herself to a wild embrace

the instant she goes into the tunnel
in which a living body gets to know
what it's like six-feet under.

ZENICA BLUES

It's snowing today, for the first
time this year, and there's a yellow
truck jack-knifed by the library:
piles of shiny pills litter the street.
Dusk gathers along the avenue
like the darkness under your eyes.
The snow will cover up miles
of rusty iron. Across the river,
rugby players in black and red uniforms
roll their own breath out before them.
A young guy with his head bowed down
shoots the wet pavement in front of him
with a video. Nothing else. You pass
by, stepping along with no love lost

•

Strange, for over a year you
haven't seen a fly here, even
in the heat of summer.
For sure there're no fish
in the river either but plenty
of gulls dive for old loaves
of bread soaked in water.
You couldn't ever see the
cemetary from here, at least
not till yesterday. Now there are

two at the top of the hill: two
grey cat-paws on the prison wall.
And things are getting clearer

•

You cover the bright bulb with
an old sheet of newspaper:
tired from the long wait,
you lie in the shadows
reading headlines.
Finally
you hear the squeal of tires
through the window:
miniature red boxing gloves
hang off the mirror in the lit
up interior

•

The way out of town is long:
the driver checks the tickets
through his glasses but
drives without them.
A jailbird shoots the breeze with a cop.
A narrow street with a container
that has CULTURAL CENTER written on it
lets out onto a square
and nothing surprises you

anymore as you see
an old man trip over a gull
on the sidewalk.

                •

We go over the bridge slowly:
a woman her face red from eczema
puts two small figs into
a straw basket full of apples.
She cranes her neck to look at
the rows of blue buildings in the fog,
so downhearted that
you know
she'll never
come back.

                •

On the hill above Rajlovac,
you move out of the sun.
Black locusts fill the bare
treetops, and a thousand crows
cover the dry grass: evenings like
this, January, 1990, you know they're
not in the mood anymore: one way or
another, they've reconciled themselves
to move along quictly and
migrate from Yugoslavia forever

•

In the café BALKAN, a local poet holds forth:
What's written in books isn't history,
it's all in the prison archives.
Last time I was here I saw
a famous émigré, everyone's
writing about him now — what
a tyrant he was. A real gentleman,
who wouldn't be, with that kind
of gold! He sat right here and drank
coffee, with no sugar. Now I'm here
and he's in an easychair on the edge
of a Swiss lake scratching his cat
and hiccuping from his name
being mentioned so much.
He had two tough dogs, though —
Danes or Dobermans, dark
jaws out to here on them, but
not killers. And before you know it
they'd be back with his dick
in their teeth, right back
to their master, the guy
everyone feels so sorry for now

•

A few miles out of Zenica
the bus goes into a sharp curve:

you feel the weight of the girl
in the seat next to you, the warmth
of her shoulder. And you see three
bouquets of roses wrapped in cellophane
held to the cold cement with scotch-tape.
Look, that won't last too long, I say,
just to make small talk.
And she nods. As if she knows

•

You look out the window of the bus:
someone's set some dried shrubs on fire—
the color of flame leaps out of the grey
and brown as kids circle around with long
sticks transfixed by the blaze

•

An icy morning at the station—
hot off the press, the newspapers
under your sweater keep you warm
It makes you even colder to look at those
two as they part with short kisses
frozen in an embrace as their
glasses collide

•

The woman in a seat near you
is talking to herself:
Fine—she says—all right,
just don't touch
All eyes turn to you
and you also turn to
see who's at fault.
Ashamed,
you turn back,
biting your shoulder

•

And on the way home:
you go into a café on the outskirts of town.
Fishermen joke around at the bar
and even though it's your first time
here, you've already seen it all:
fishermen with yellow boots up to their hips
and giant bottles of METAXA lined up
at the bar, so big
you could easily hug them.
Maybe you're someone else,
someone you don't even know.
If you kept thinking about it, just
the thought would devastate you

•

You find yourself in the
toilet with
a Sarajevo rocker
Jewish
and while you take
a leak together you bond
in perfect male solidarity:
That's how it is, says the Jewish guy,
and you nod in agreement even though
it isn't like that
nothing's for sure
except two circumcisions
by the flushing bowl

•

Without you everything
in this town will still be the same.
Or almost—you reassure yourself,
like when you use a huge wooden
match to light a cigarette.
So remember a few details,
like the rattling of silver rings,
or your glass bowls.
And all the instances that
mercilessly surround your
AWKWARDNESS: the clash
of teeth in a kiss, for instance,
before you recognize the

ghostly rattling of bones
in the silence
that you might have imagined
like your fear of dying in winter
when the laundry freezes on the line
and the ribs of numb undershirts crack

DATES

He was killed January 17th, 1994 —
Every day from then on
he's been dead

he's dead today too

it's Friday
February 24th, 1995.

Every day I have a transcendental experience —
When I go to the bathroom at night
I notice a shadow rising in the mirror
over my left shoulder

it isn't mine

I turn and
what do I see?

My eyes open
in sleep —
a raven has landed on my table
and in a human voice says:
Cherries will be ripe in Sarajevo the 17th of May

I heard
and I'm waiting

AN INTERVIEW WITH SEMEZDIN MEHMEDINOVIĆ BY AMMIEL ALCALAY

AMMIEL ALCALAY: Most of the Eastern Europe writers Americans are familiar with emerged from a generation prior to yours and were looked at as dissidents of one kind or another within the context of the cold war. How do you see your generation?

SEMEZDIN MEHMEDINOVIĆ: I remember well the period in which any interest in Eastern European writing was exclusively related to ideology, and this is something that I clearly experienced as someone writing from the perspective of Eastern Europe. The work of those considered "dissidents" in the west was promoted. In addition to any inherent interest in one literature or another simply for its quality, it's also very natural for there to be extra-literary reasons for its dissemination beyond a local context. If the reasons for publishing such writers in America, for example, were based completely on ideology, I think that, again, in the case of America, there has been a positive change in which the American model now wants to include all the world's cultures in it. The way New York is constructed, for example, there is this ambition to demonstrate a plurality of everything, from food and ethnic neighborhoods to the fact that you have writers here from everywhere, many of whom write in their own language while still maintaining a sense of presence here. In this sense, I can see a dramatic difference in my being here now, let's say, and the phenomenon of someone like Brodsky in a different period. The reason why I find this so valuable is that I see a process taking place here that is diametrically opposed to what happened in Sarajevo. We have to remember that Sarajevo was one of the few European cities that would be hard to categorize in terms of a "national" literature. National literatures exist in all the major European centers, from Moscow to London—there is a national English literature, a national Russian literature, and so on. This is a very different distinction than the impact these centers have now felt through the influx of new immigrants or former colonial subjects. In the case of Bosnia, you simply could not say that the literature written in Sarajevo or Bosnia-Hercegovina was Bosnian or Croatian or Serbian. But this is precisely what has happened as a result of the war, that on the borders of culture all kinds of divisions and separations have been made. When you force these kinds of sharp divisions—in this case within the same language—the results are bloody. The best of what I see here demonstrates a model that can only benefit all cultures.

AA: As a translator, I had a very hard time finding a space for Bosnian culture until the war broke out; I realized that in order to present a writer like you, or other earlier or contemporary Bosnian writers, I would first have to introduce readers to the present situation through dramatic and timely journalistic texts about the war, in order for American readers to simply begin familiarizing themselves with the idea that such a thing as a Bosnian perspective actually exists. How do you deal with the fact that maybe now you no longer represent the cold war dissident, but that your function here is tied to that of being some kind of a representative of the war?

SM: It's natural that light has to be shed on something for it to become interesting. That light can, as in this case, be the war, or something completely unrelated to anything. Someone can show up on TV—and I am not using this example here by chance—with a seemingly ordinary story that suddenly circles the globe. Television, in this sense, has become this dangerous contagious and, in some cases, blessed medium, which focuses attention on things. Unfortunately, interest for the literature and culture of Bosnia-Hercegovina was primarily elicited through the horrors of war. Since the media bombarded the whole world with this story, it stands to reason that some further curiosity would develop—first of all about the war itself, and things written about the war. In the first phase, as you mentioned, this was more related to journalism through the work of war correspondents simply because of a need for information. As the public familiarized themselves with this information, a need for more sophisticated and complex forms of representation presents itself and the space for literature, film, music and other forms opens up. But as someone coming from a smaller language and culture, I cannot make light of this first opening because I do think that once there is a base of social and political information, people will gravitate towards wanting to reach a more metaphysical plane that can be seen, for instance, through poetry. Out of such encounters a fuller picture of the culture can begin to emerge. For now we are still generally seeing only one layer, the layer most concerned with the present political situation.

AA: Can you say something about your own generation? What were your influences?

SM: My generation follows the generation that actively produced the war. That generation would include someone like Radovan Karadžić, on the demonic side if you will, and someone like Abdulah Sidran, the great poet of Sarajevo and well known for film scripts he wrote such as *Remember Dolly Bell, When Father Was Away on Business,* and Ademir Kenović's latest film, *Closed Circle.* So in such an equation Sidran, of course, would be on the angelic side, if we can make such black-and-white distinctions which I think, in this case, we can. This was a generation that grew up on Russian cultural models; Yugoslavia, as we know, was a socialist country in which there was a very intense presence of Russian culture. My generation came of age when that kind of socialism had become Socialism-lite, when the ideological pressures had eased. It was hard to get put in jail for going against the authorities in this period. My own experience was that you could go to trial but it would really end up as a farce that more than anything only liberated young narcissists from any responsibility to actually criticize the power structure in any deep or threatening way. Nevertheless, this was clearly an anti-military generation, totally unprepared for war in the sense of picking up a gun and fighting. And this is the generation that lost this war. The late 1970s and 1980s saw a great interest in comic book art, rock music and film, that's what me and my generation educated ourselves on. First of all European film—Italian and German, Antonioni, Wenders and so on. But rock'n roll was certainly a major influence on us, primarily as a gathering point that produced a common aesthetic. During the 1980s in Sarajevo, the same sources motivated artists, musicians, writers, photographers and performers. That ten-year period, actually, was a kind of love affair with the city, and participants in the scene represented—or at least that's how it seemed—an urban ideology. The most genuine representatives of everything that went on then are members of the band *No Smoking*, a band that ultimately splintered into two parts, one in Sarajevo and the other in Belgrade. At the end of the war, the Sarajevo version of *No Smoking* came out with a CD of love songs, while the Belgrade version of *No Smoking* came out with an album of war songs; for them, the war wasn't over.

AA: What was your stance and those of people you were connected with to other cultural centers in the former Yugoslavia?

SM: There was intense communication between like-minded people because we were a generation essentially brought up with similar aesthetic interests. So it was natural to have both friendly and professional relationships throughout the former Yugoslavia for readings, cultural events, little magazines, literary journals, concerts, film and theater festivals and so on. My generation also clearly distinguished ourselves from an earlier one in our transparency—we were simply fed up with the kind of obscure, metaphorical style that was the dominant model. We were completely attuned to the exterior world, and wanted to make ourselves understood. We had a real need for precision, with some belief that if we could put on paper precisely what was in the outside world that, in itself, would convey the emotional potential indispensable to poetry. We thought such a method would already contain specific feelings so that we chose associations that seemed to us more authentic than the often forced efforts of our predecessors to dredge things up from an interior world.

AA: When did you begin to differentiate between those sources and terms of reference in your situation that could be characterized as specifically Bosnian and things that were happening in the rest of the country?

SM: Actually you are asking me if there was a point at which I could differentiate myself from people who, in quite short shrift, would be holding a gun to my head. I think this happened quite early on and, in some sense, encompasses all the time that I have been engaged as a writer. It starts with the language itself. I come from a language that, stubbornly, remains undefined. It still isn't defined—the only reason for defining it at this point is ideological. Now it is the Bosnian language because it has to be preserved from the monopoly of another nation/language, in this case Serbian. I always felt a kind of covert monopoly by another national entity even though this never really affected my own work personally since I never allowed myself to recognize it. But it did create a feeling of uneasiness. On the other hand, even though I was clearly aware of such things in the 1980s, I would never have jumped to the conclusion that things could go in the direction they did. If I shared similar aesthetic interests with friends in Belgrade or Zagreb or Ljubljana or Bosnia-Hercegovina, it was quite another thing to imagine this same person turning into a post-modern sniper and shooting at me from the Jewish Cemetary. But that, unfortunately, is what happened. At the same time, I think that by the mid 1980s one could already predict the war. I remember a radio program that we did called "Waste Land" and we talked about the certainty of war. Amongst ourselves we really did feel that such a war was unavoidable, during the period of mass demonstrations and so forth. These demonstrations of course, relate to the rise of Milošević and the whole question of Kosovo.

AA: What was your awareness and that of your contemporaries regarding the situation in Kosovo?

SM: We were very engaged in the issue of Kosovo.

AA: Were you in touch with writers there?

SM: Absolutely, and we were very involved in what was going on. We wrote extensively about it and, of course, we also went there. There was a Writer's Colony there, for instance, that I spent time at. We constantly were involved in various activities to pronounce the fact that a culture had to be protected, in this case, Albanian culture. I remember after our radio show people were convinced that this was some kind of a fantasy. I must say that I don't think I even fully accepted the truth of it consciously. This period also fully demonstrated a kind of deep sinking into amorality. On a social level, for example, there was enormous promiscuity. Communication between people became very contentious as external issues dominated and invaded personal relations. On the everyday level, there was a kind of black-market consciousness that went into operation. Even if we think of these phenomena as less important, the point is that we were all, in some sense, engaged in this war atmosphere. We commented on everything that was taking place in Kosovo, but with a belief that it would never get beyond state terrorism.

AA: Did you already feel differences then, let's say, between friends in Belgrade?

SM: Of course. This had a great effect on people. The crisis in Kosovo provoked open debate over national differences —this process resulted in polemics in Sarajevo in which many writers were involved. One of the main reasons for these polemics had to do with the battle that raged between Serbs and Croats over editorial positions in publishing houses and literary journals. If there were too many representative of one group, then changes were made. There was a backlash against Croatians in Sarajevo, for example, since they held a higher number of editorial positions. Prominent people began to move: several very important writers and intellectuals from Sarajevo actually moved, paradoxically, to Belgrade, and others from Belgrade moved to Sarajevo. It was in this kind of confusion that everything was cooked up to create the kinds of frustrating situations that were often brought out in cultural terms and through literary polemics.

AA: It seems to me that your generation has quite a different take on things than, say, intellectuals in the former Yugoslavia who came of age in the late 1960s. With them, I see a kind of liberalism that is curiously removed from politics, partly, I think, from a disgust with Yugoslavia's hypcrisy regarding the non-Aligned movement, the third world, and so on. At the same time, such liberals seemed quite unaware of what that was all about, and that Yugoslavia was, in many ways, part of that third world and not as close to Western Europe as they might have liked to think. How do you see this?

SM: My perspective here has to begin from this: if I look at the literature of Bosnia-Hercegovina and then I look at the literature written in Sarajevo, you can see that within the framework of one language, very diverse kinds of phenomena come into play. You have, for example, the Sephardic writer Isak Samokovlija, who at this stage might no longer even be considered part of the mix since the borders between cultures have been moved and imposed. Where is one to place him? He is neither Bosnian, Croatian or Serbian, but being Jewish and Bosnian and partaking of all these cultures, he truly is Bosnian. If a writer like Samokovlija is not considered part of Bosnian literature, then this means we are again faced with a different kind of monopoly over language. So, you have Bosnian writing; you have Serbian writing which has its own external reference point in Belgrade or other parts of Serbia, and you have Croatian writing which also has a central reference point in Zagreb. What I see of great value in my generation, and what somehow has to be preserved, is this kind of inextricable connectedness and diversity. There was absolutely no nationalist omen or agenda hidden between the lines of this literature, because if there was the whole body of that literature would be immeasurably impoverished — in the past, in what is being written now, and in what will be done in the future to this past. As soon as you begin dividing up cultural borders, you present a great danger to other cultures — in this case my own, and the one that I want to consider myself a part of in better times to come. Because this Bosnian culture is inclusive, it includes the Bosnian Franciscan tradition, the Muslim sufi tradition, and the Sephardic Jewish tradition; this is all part of my culture, as well as Goethe, so that limitations can't be imposed. I think that the generation you mention succumbed very easily to the imposition of limitations.

AA: It seems to me important to find out why it was so easy for such intellectuals to accept these kinds of limitations. I'm not speaking here of the nationalist intellectuals who fueled the whole war project; I refer to people who were even in the opposition but whose opposition was not based on any strong positions. The cultural resistance in Bosnia, for instance, showed precisely how strong the bonds of this mixed culture were.

SM: At this moment, for instance, all the intellectuals and all the cultural institutions in Belgrade are working on only one project: to equalize blame for the war on all sides. And this is a remarkable process, because this intoxication with nationalism, connected with militarism and some kind of feudal urge for conquest has infiltrated everything. It is very difficult to find a response to this fantastic hypnosis. The cultural resistance in Sarajevo was so strong precisely because of this cultural mix that has always existed. There, certainly during the first two years of the war, there were enough people of all groups who underwent the exact same constant threat of annihilation, and the only people who had time for ideology were those on the sidelines who didn't have to deal with the details of everyday survival under such conditions. And I don't think the situation in Croatia regarding this is any better, with some very notable exceptions. Usually, in these so-called local wars, you simply have people with rifles, and there's no time for writing or culture or art. But here we had the opposite: shells were falling, and film festivals were organized. We didn't have any paper but, somehow, we still published books. When there wasn't paper for little magazines, we turned them into radio shows.

AA: How do you see your own work from before the war, during the war and after it. Did things change, or did the events simply affirm things you had already been doing?

SM: The war brought a very specific state of being with it. For me, it was the first time in my life that I had a lot of time and it gave me the chance to work. I wrote. It was the first time in my life that I could just write, so I was very happy about that, and fulfilled because of it. The war also brought with it something I didn't have before. Before the war I was filled with doubt, stops and starts, not sure about my writing — was there a purpose to it, what was the purpose of it? During the war I saw that it really did have a purpose because that primal instinct of the storyteller continuing even though the flames were all around came into play. I could see how people reacted to what came out. At first there was a passion for information, the desire to inform the world about what was going on here developed into a kind of reflex among people. But when everyone realized that dialogue with the outer world had ceased, there was an even greater need to interpret what was going on here to ourselves. And this is a way in which writers were truly enriched, by returning to this primary function. Things were read. So it turned out that the doubts I had in my work were not grounded on anything. The relationship between reader and writer was very complete.

AA: You stayed in Sarajevo until the war, for all intents and purposes, stopped. Why did you leave, and how do you see your work here?

SM: I feel autistic here, with one foot in Washington where I live now, and another in Sarajevo. It has been an extremely valuable experience, though, to be able to get such a different perspective of things there. I have the impression that I am more present there now than when I was actually there, because then I was just mired in the situation. One of the reasons I left is simply the exhaustion of living under those camp conditions. I had become completely unproductive. Things closed in on a small circle of intellectuals from which there was no exit. People just started tearing each other apart, like-minded people who had worked together on various projects just lost their patience. You simply couldn't work cooperatively anymore, either between groups or among people working on different things. From the exhaustion of this collective survival, I think people just had to turn back on each other as some kind of a defense mechanism to regain a sense of autonomy. As opposed to the beginning of the war and during the war, it became impossible to work with anyone. Again, I think this was just a case of sheer exhaustion. I also left for political reasons, because of what is going on now in this monstruous hybrid political structure that's been imposed and accepted. I couldn't simply watch as people collaborated in their own demise and just swallow it. Criminals who shelled Sarajevo and were en route to seeking asylum somewhere as an escape from being put on trial in the Hague are now serving as ambassadors in the Bosnian government. People involved in the destruction of historical towns and the killing of civilians now serve on the government's commission for Human Rights. Throughout the war, Sarajevo was a synonym for Bosnia-Hercegovina while Pale was a kind of military barrack annexed to Belgrade and you couldn't mention it as part of Bosnia but only as some kind of terrorist enclave within Bosnia. Now these people have been completely legitimized, as legitimate as the government in Sarajevo. As dubious as they are, they have now cast a shadow on the Bosnian government itself which, after all, helped legitimize them by bringing them in. So war criminals are brought into the circle of power while a hero like Marko Vešović, a Montenegran poet and literary critic who stayed in Sarajevo throughout the war, is being threatened with expulsion. So by the end of 1995, I really felt like I had lost my cover, that I remained, in some sense, completely unprotected. I had the feeling that public opinion no longer really existed in the city and that if I were simply taken off the map, no one would even react. Having survived the war, this was not a good feeling to have. The people in my generation—who were dragged in to the war, and many of them killed—have proved to be the real losers because they were defending a way of life that didn't stand a chance, at least not in the short run. In the long run, though, I'm absolutely certain that the practice of cultural division and racism doesn't stand a chance because there is a law of equilibrium in which things come back to themselves. We will get back to a point at which this mixture of cultures creates a whole, rather than the kind of fragmentation that turns into the ideological farce we are witnessing now. Presently, everything is seen through an ideological grid. Even a writer like Ivo Andrić, former Yugoslavia's Nobel Prize winner, is seen through this perspective as a "controversial" writer, simply for ideological reasons, even though no one can escape his influence. He is probably the most manipulated since he was, in fact, a Croat who wrote about Bosnia but was adopted by the Serbs in the centrism of former Yugoslavia. The Croats, actually, never include him in official Croatian literature, You can see how complex this gets. The line during the war became that Andrić thought of Bosnia as a country filled with hatred and dark forces but this is one sentence taken out of context in a passage where he is talking about someone's journey into a kind of provincial hole and he hears a voice proclaiming his existential dilemna. But the writers who directed this ideological attack took this as proof of Bosnia's dark past in the crudest and most simplistic ways possible. Even Danilo Kiš, one of the most lucid interpreters of Balkan nationalism, adopted this cliche in his essays on Bosnia. If he had read Andrić as carefully as he claimed, he would have seen that he skipped a few pages of the history of this land and that this cliche simply came out of an ideological need for one form of authority to close off any other ways of thinking about this place.

AA: What are some of the sources of your work?

I mentioned Danilo Kiš, who was very important to me. During the war, in particular, I read his work on poetics intensively. I must say that a lot of what I read before the war did not mean as much to me later. Things that could be classified as post-modern, for instance, and which certainly influenced me and my generation, really lacked a moral dimension and during the war this lack had very specific and concrete effects on us. Personally, I think film plays a bigger role in my work than writing itself. If I think of it in terms of the erotic relationship between what others create and what I am then sanctioned or inspired to do, film and the plastic arts mean more to me. There are books, of course, that I can never stop reading but the things that spur on my own work tend to be in other media. In terms of writing, I find the essay form draws me, maybe because I am interested in the whole question of form and the mixing of poetry, prose and journalism that characterizes so much of the work I did during the war. I am very conscious of the disintegration of my reality, the extinction of a whole world, and now I am writing a book about the disappearance of that world through the dissolution of one family. I do this not because I believe that if something is written down it can somehow be preserved from oblivion, but rather because I have come to believe that freedom only exists in the space of memory.

Washington Square Park, New York, January 1998

Translated by Ammiel Alcalay

ABOUT THE AUTHOR

Semezdin Mehmedinovic was born in Tuzla, Bosnia in 1960 and is the author of four books. In 1993 he was co-writer and co-director, together with Benjamin Filipović, of *Mizaldo*, one of the first Bosnian films shot during the war. The film was presented at the Berlin Film Festival in 1994, and won the first prize at the Mediterranean Festival in Rome the following year. He, his wife and their child left Bosnia and came to the U.S. as political refugees in 1996.